D0962415

BLESSINGS AND EXPRESSIONS OF
HOPE FOR THE NEW MILLENNIUM

PRAYERS *for a*
THOUSAND
YEARS

EDITED BY

ELIZABETH ROBERTS AND ELIAS AMIDON

HarperSanFrancisco
A Division of HarperCollinsPublishers

HarperSanFrancisco and the editors, in association with The Basic Foundation, a not-for-profit organization whose primary mission is reforestation, will facilitate the planting of two trees for every one tree used in the manufacture of this book.

A TREE CLAUSE BOOK

FIRST EDITION

Illustrations by Kathleen Edwards
Book design by Laura Lindgren
Set in Berkeley

Library of Congress Cataloging-in-Publication Data
Prayers for a thousand years : blessings and expressions of hope for the new
    millennium / edited by Elizabeth Roberts and Elias Amidon.—1st ed.
        p.   cm.
    Includes index.
    ISBN 0–06–066875–X (pbk.)
    1. Millennium. 2. Prayers. I. Roberts, Elizabeth J. II. Amidon, Elias.
BT891.P73 1999
291.4'33—dc21
                                                                98–43252

99 00 01 02 03 RRD(H) 10 9 8 7 6 5 4 3 2

This book is dedicated to our friends and mentors:

Sulak Sivaraksa, Thai advocate for human rights,
Oscar Motomura, Brazilian businessman and visionary,
Murshida Sitara Brutnell, spiritual leader of the Sufi Way.

CONTENTS

Contents

6. THIS HOLY EARTH *185*

7. PRAYERS OF SOLIDARITY AND JUSTICE *229*

8. REFLECTIONS ON POLITICS, ECONOMICS, AND MORALITY 269

9. PARABLES OF OUR TIME 299

Contents

10. WE THE PEOPLE *329*

Contents

THANKS

"Give thanks and praises!"
BOB MARLEY

All thanks to the One Gracious Spirit for this book!
Thanks to the trees that gave their bodies for its pages!
Thanks to the trucks who carried them!
Thanks to the printing machines,
the stock handlers in the warehouse, and the booksellers!
Thanks to you good reader!

Thanks to the many souls who sent prayers, poems, stories:
invocations for a new millennium
calling forth what we love.
Thank you for knowing it makes a difference.
Whether your writing is printed here or not,
you shared in this creation,
this millennial song echoing down the centuries.
Thanks and praises!

Thanks to Ruth Merriman who made it happen—the faxes, the phones, the correspondence and files—who held it all together with implacable good spirits, blessing us and the project with her steadiness. Thanks to Joe Richey, poet, editor, and translator, for his generosity and skill, and for spreading the call to Latin America and to a world of poets. Thanks to park ranger and novelist Pat Walsh for inviting indigenous and spiritual leaders, environmentalists and teachers, at the same time she was saving prairie dog habitat. Thanks to Amy Bright for opening the call to young people and their teachers so enthusiastically, to Staci Caplan for overseeing the mailings with a joyful spirit, and to Ben Levi for keeping us and our computers sane.

We are especially grateful to our editors, John Loudon and Karen Levine, for their commitment to this project and their kindness to us. Thanks also to Judy Durham and Terri Leonard at Harper San Francisco, to our agents, Michael Carlisle and Matt Bialer, and to Donna Gianoulis and Danielle La Porte of The Next Level, for helping us navigate unfamiliar waters.

And thanks once again to Michael Baier, friend, writer, and raconteur, for believing in us. This book would not exist without him.

Finally, we wish to extend deep thanks to each of the women and men on the Honorary Council. They understood the power of invocation, gave their good names in solidarity with the project, advised us as they were able, and shared their contacts and address books. Their lives and work bear witness to the spirit of *Prayers for a Thousand Years*.

Elizabeth Roberts and Elias Amidon
Colorado, 1999

HONORARY COUNCIL

Dr. Angeles Arrien
Dr. Ysaye Barnwell
Dr. Joan Borysenko
David Brower
Ellen Burstyn
Bhiksuni Pema Chodron
Larry Dossey, M.D.
Ven. Maha Ghosananda
Bernard Glassman, Roshi
Dr. Jane Goodall
Dr. Joan Halifax
Dr. Vincent Harding
Dr. Jean Houston
Fr. Thomas Keating
Jack Kornfield
Bishop Labayan
Winona LaDuke
Arvol Looking Horse
Chief Oren Lyons

Wangari Maathai
Dr. Joanna Macy
Dean James Parks Morton
Oscar Motomura
Dr. Robert Muller
don Alejandro Cirilo Perez
   Oxlaj
Dr. Bernice Reagon
Rachel Naomi Remen, M.D.
Dr. Rosemary Radford Ruether
Rabbi Zalman Schachter-
   Shalomi
Malidoma & Sobonfu Somé
Br. David Steindl-Rast
Gloria Steinem
Achaan Sulak Sivaraksa
Archbishop Desmond Tutu
Abdurahman Wahid
Jim Wallis

INTRODUCTION

Anything we love can be saved.
ALICE WALKER

Prayers for a Thousand Years is a testament to what we love in this world. It is an expression of what we wish to save and invoke for the generations that will follow us. The prayers, blessings, warnings, and reflections that fill this book have been offered by people of diverse faiths and cultures in honor of our mutual entry into the third millennium of the common era (c.e.). They represent a testament of hope in a time beset with fears and uncertainty—a testament that may come to pass in the centuries ahead, if we remember its message.

The great majority of these pieces were written specifically for this book. All the authors represented here are alive at this historical moment, members of the generations of us who now cross over the millennium threshold together.

But this book is more than a collective "toast" to the world on New Year's Eve. The enduring themes sung by this chorale of voices will resonate through the years of the new millennium as expressions of what matters most to us—justice, love, compassion, democracy, beauty, community, gratefulness. And above all—*life!* The voices here sing of life's recurring resurrection from fear and hatred. They sing of hope in the face of all the tragedies we humans have brought down upon ourselves. And they ask us to remember. Remember what makes life worth living. Remember that caring for the well-being of others is the same as caring for ourselves. Remember that this beautiful earth, our home, is sacred.

The turn of the century and the millennium is a fitting time to call forth these reminders.

WHAT IS THE SIGNIFICANCE OF THE MILLENNIUM?

The "millennium moment" and the millennium itself are events of the imagination. They are, and will be, what we make of them. There is no cosmological clock that marks the turning of the second millennium C.E. into the third, no astronomical event, no chorus of angels. It is, in fact, an arbitrary moment based generally (but not exactly) on the birth of Christ two thousand years ago. While there are other contemporary calendar systems in use—most notably the Islamic, Hebrew, Buddhist, and Chinese calendars—the "common era" has become the generally accepted standard for international cooperation. As such, the counting of its cycles resonates throughout the world, reminding us of our work together, of the ongoing drama of the communities of nations seeking to live in harmony on the same planet. The turning of the millennium has become an occasion for people all over the globe to consider the long sweep of the ages as we begin counting together a "new" span of time stretching one thousand years ahead.

One thousand winters. One thousand springs. Implicit in this contemplation of time are many provocative questions: What will this next thousand years bring for humans and for all life on earth? Will human life in the deep future fulfill our spiritual and creative potential, or will this world become a mechanical and soulless place dominated by fear and oppression? What do we want to be true? What are we willing to do to achieve that truth?

At the turn of the millennium a thousand years ago, Europeans felt great anxiety for the imminent end of the world. Similar apocalyptic dreams seem to trouble postmodern civilization—witness the plethora of films and books describing Armageddon-like natural disasters, invasions of extraterrestrials, and wars of total annihilation. For many people, especially the young, faith in the future is weakening. We are living through the end of a tumultuous century of change and war, a time that provokes feelings of widespread anxiety and cynicism. But such a time also evokes within and around us opportunities for hope and compassionate action. We are called to be *more* human—or, as Abraham Lincoln put it, to be "the better angels of our nature"—to manifest our potential for tolerance, respect, and kindness. It is this call we hear in the voices of this book.

HOW THIS BOOK CAME ABOUT

For nearly a decade we, the editors, have been guiding small groups of men and women into the Great Basin Desert in Utah to enable them to experience three- and four-day periods of spiritually focused solitude. During this solo time, people have the opportunity to contemplate the meaning and direction of their lives. These experiences are modern-day rites of passage for people of all ages—adults entering mid-life, young people coming of age, and people marking a marriage or divorce, considering a career change, or facing a life-threatening illness. Over time we have learned that the most powerful and successful rites of passage are guided by *a deep articulation of intention*. Why are you doing this? we ask. What are you seeking? And what do you want us to pray for as you sit alone out there? These questions stir ever-deeper answers. When things get rough during the solo time—whether due to windstorm or rain, hunger or loneliness—each person calls upon his or her own spoken intention, the "root prayer" that reminds participants why they are out there and what they are seeking to realize in their lives.

One day we saw that the approach of the millennium moment represented, on a global scale, a collective rite of passage. As we are all too aware, the rate of cultural, technological, political, and psychological change is overwhelming people and societies everywhere. Cultures are having to let go of old forms and ways of being and enter a "threshold" stage, a time of unknowing and gestation, while the seeds of our collective future take root. The historical experience of this millennium moment may encompass several decades. It is a time, as are all rites of passage, to slow down and ask ourselves what we value from the past and what we wish to invoke for the years ahead. It is a time to open ourselves to inspiration and to directions we may not have imagined.

With that realization came the first outlines of this project. Having collected two previous volumes of prayers from around the world—*Earth Prayers* (1991) and *Life Prayers* (1996)—we knew the process would be both enchanting and difficult. But we had no idea it would meet with the range of support and encouragement that it has. This project touched people deeply—people from diverse cultures and faiths. Soon we formed an Honorary Council of distinguished leaders and teachers (see page xv) who gave their blessings to the project.

We sent out invitations to over three thousand people around the world. In each letter we included these words:

> The energy of our visions and intentions can blow like a wind through the next millennium, influencing the imaginations and actions of those who come after us. If we imagine there is a chance that our people—all people— might one day learn to live in beauty and kindness with each other and with the rest of the world's life, then we can ask: What might we pray for now, at this potent moment in history, to help invoke this possible future?

These invitations to participate by sending a written prayer or message to the future made their way to the offices of presidents and prime ministers, to death row in San Quentin prison, to a classroom of children in New Hampshire, to a fifteen-year-old ex-soldier in Sierra Leone, to poets in Latin America and native elders in Canada, to Catholic nuns in China and environmentalists in California. We were seeking people whose love for the world was stronger than their disappointment.

Once the invitations were sent, for the better part of a year our mailbox, fax machine, and email were blessed with a steady stream of prayers, philosophic reflections, poems, guidance, and advice—over fourteen hundred submissions in all. It was deeply moving to read these offerings each day; as the news told stories of murder, war, injustice, pollution, and ignorance, our mailbox told stories of people's faith and their determination to reach beyond the distrust of differences.

In the end, about two-thirds of the submissions came from English-speaking countries. Yet even with this culturally weighted response, the selections in this book are remarkably diverse. There are pieces from thirty-one countries on all six continents. There are prayers from Christians, Jews, Muslims, Hindus, Buddhists, Jains, Taoists, Confucians, Mayans, Maoris, Africans, Sioux, Eyak, Australian Aborigines, and many other ethnic and religious groups.

The final process of selection was painful. A great many wonderful prayers had to be cut for want of space, or because they repeated themes expressed by others. Gradually the structure of the book's ten parts emerged from the material itself. And now the book you hold in your hands holds the strong voices of these men and women, holds their aspirations for a just and beautiful world. It is their gift to you and to all of us. May they be heard!

HOW TO USE THIS BOOK

You might try reading one of these prayers before each meal, like a grace. You might read one at daybreak each day, upon rising. You might read them at Christmas or Hanukkah, Easter or Thanksgiving, at the solstices and equinoxes, or at other religious or secular holidays to call forth the deep aspirations of the human family. Of course, they are very appropriate for focusing intentions during the many millennium observances that will take place during the millennium moment—the years 1999, 2000, and 2001.

But these are prayers for a *thousand* years, not just three. We humans need a lot of reminding. In these pages we may find touchstones to help us remember what we know in our hearts but cannot always speak.

This book can be read silently, its meanings touching you in that silence. But most of the written words printed here call to be spoken aloud. By speaking them aloud we connect to the oral traditions that are far older than the written word—the oral traditions of poetry and chanting, parable and song that guided our ancestors for millennia before us. Our hope is that these prayers, along with others like them, will be spoken and shared wherever people gather to work for a better world.

Most important, by speaking these words aloud you give them life. For whether poetry or prose, religious or secular, these pieces are "prayers" in the original meaning of the word—that is, "entreaties." Some entreat God or Buddha, Allah or Krishna, but certainly all of them entreat us. They entreat us to awaken. They entreat us to listen. They entreat us to be kind. Spoken, sometimes just whispered, they achieve an intimacy that holds a deep power to move us. Try it. The communion they offer is the heart of real communication and of caring community.

Part 1

VISIONS *of* HOPE

And all shall be well
and all shall be well
and all manner of thing shall be well.
JULIAN OF NORWICH

Prayers for a Thousand Years begins with visions of hope. It is upon visions such as these, and upon the intentions they reveal, that a new world can be built. The visioning process is not a task that is done once and then forgotten; again and again we must attempt to restate our hopes and reimagine the possibilities open to us. We must continually call forth visions, even if they are just glimpses, of how we might align our lives more closely with our dreams and values.

The prayers in Part 1 focus beyond the immediate and real problems of our time, offering images of hope that will support us on the longer journey. But this hope is not Pollyanna sentimentality. The men and women who offer their prayers in this section have witnessed the suffering caused by fear, greed, and anger and have reached deep within themselves and within our common humanity to find resilience and patience. "I am filled with hope for the future," writes Archbishop Desmond Tutu. "In spite of much to the contrary, the world is becoming a kinder, safer place." This is radical optimism. And it is heartening, giving us courage to persevere in the work that calls us.

In the archbishop's words, notice the phrase "in spite of much to the contrary." This phrase reveals an important quality of unsentimental hope: it is not blind to the darker sides of our nature. As we look in the millennium mirror, we must admit that the human species is capable of both nobility and horror. We cannot ignore the horror and pretend that all is well as we walk into the future. We know we carry our failings along with our dreams. Yet this knowledge does not have to paralyze us with foreboding or despair. Our individual destinies and the destiny of life on earth are by no means sealed. The great spiritual traditions of the world understand this, and each in its own way seeks to reveal hope and meaning in the midst of the profound changes experienced by all societies.

The most compelling visions offer images that we can *see* in our mind's eye. True visions are not simply ideas or goals; they carry layers of meaning and intention that communicate more directly than a corporate five-year plan. Listen here to a young Cambodian, Chath Piersath, praying for his war-torn country:

> There will be playgrounds instead of war zones.
> There will be more schools instead of brothels and night-
> clubs.
> The children will sing songs of joy instead of terror.
> They will learn how to read love instead of hate.

Such images communicate a vision that touches and motivates. The new world we build will emerge from individual glimpses of a more just and beautiful world being created step by step. To facilitate that creation, we need to let go of preconceived notions of what is possible or customary and allow ourselves to imagine our deepest dreams come true. "Everywhere the transformation will look different," Bill McKibben tells us, "just as spring comes to each spot with subtly different signs and vestiges."

This is our work: to dare to envision a more just and beautiful tomorrow and to be glad for the diverse ways spring comes to our world. The voices rising from Part 1 foretell the coming of spring, gently assuring us that "all shall be well, and all shall be well, and all manner of thing shall be well."

5

Look back from where we have come.
The path was at times an open road of joy,
at others a steep and bitter track of stones and pain.

How could we know the joy without the suffering?
And how could we endure the suffering but that we are
    warmed and carried on the breast of God?

6

We are His children, created in His image, made for love and laughter, caring and sharing. I am filled with hope for the future. In spite of much to the contrary, the world is becoming a kinder, safer place. It is God's world, and He is in charge. His gifts of goodness and kindness, reason and understanding, science and discovery are showered upon us. Revel in these gifts, enjoy them, share them, and this new millennium will become a highway of peace and prosperity for all.

Most Rev. Desmond M. Tutu
Archbishop Emeritus, South Africa

We are about to enter the 15 millionth millennium of the universe.
We are about to enter the 4.5 millionth millennium of the earth.
We are about to enter the 4 millionth millennium of life.
We are about to enter the 2,600 millennium of humans.
We are about to enter the 3rd millennium of the common era.

We are who we are today because of all that has existed before us. We carry in our bodies and spirits the struggles and changes, joys and sorrows, loves and hates that have occurred throughout all time.

We are called to live with the knowledge and awareness that we are a part of all that is and that our decisions have an affect on the quality of life for all beings. We are called to live this connectedness that exists between all members of creation. We are called to put our hands upon creation and speak to it in words and touch, telling it how lovely it is because it cannot remember. We are called to remember loveliness for one another until each of us can remember, believe, and live in love.

Sr. Mary Goergen, O.S.F.
Assisi Heights, Minnesota

May a good vision catch me
    May a benevolent vision take hold of me, and move me
May a deep and full vision come over me,
    and burst open around me
May a luminous vision inform me, enfold me.
May I awaken into the story that surrounds,
May I awaken into the beautiful story.
May the wondrous story find me;
May the wildness that makes beauty arise between two lovers
    arise beautifully between my body and the body of this land,
    between my flesh and the flesh of this earth,
    here and now,
    on this day,
May I taste something sacred.

David Abram
Ecologist and author,
Northwest Coast of North America

*   *   *

The Great Whale, the Record Keeper for time before, time now, time ahead, told me as one of her kinsfolk that everything that exists, including our Earth Mother, is going to return to the perfection that they are, in the uppermost and highest heaven. We can now celebrate the "Age of Cherishing Waters" that is in the time ahead. So Be It!

Rangimarie Turuki Rose Pere
Te Pikinga Aio, New Zealand

I Dream . . . that on 1 January 2000 the whole world will stand still in prayer, awe, and gratitude for our beautiful, heavenly Earth and for the miracle of human life.

I Dream . . . that young and old, rich and poor, black and white, peoples from North and South, from East and West, from all beliefs and cultures will join their hands, minds, and hearts in an unprecedented, universal bimillennium celebration of life.

I Dream . . . that during the year 2000 innumerable celebrations and events will take place all over the globe to gauge the long road traveled by humanity, to study our mistakes, and to plan the feats still to be accomplished for the full flowering of the human race in peace, justice, and happiness.

I Dream . . . that the celebration of the millennium will be devoted by all humans, nations, and institutions to unparalleled thinking, action, inspiration, determination, and love to solve our remaining problems and to achieve a peaceful, united human family on Earth.

I Dream . . . that the third millennium will be declared and made Humanity's First Millennium of Peace.

Robert Muller
Former Assistant Secretary General
of the United Nations, Chancellor Emeritus,
United Nations University for Peace, Costa Rica

Source of Time and Space
Avinu Malkeyinu!

10

From infinity draw down to us
The great renewal
And attune us to Your intent
So that Wisdom, Your daughter
Flow into our awareness
To awaken us to see ahead
So we help instead of harm.

May all the devices we make use of
Be sparing and protecting of Your creation.

Help us
To set right what we have debased
To heal what we have made ill
To care for and to restore what we have injured.

Bless our Earth, our home
And show us all how to care for her
So that we might live Your promise given to our forebears,
To live heavenly days
Right here on this Earth.

May all beings
Whom You have fashioned
Become aware that it is You
Who has given them being.

May we realize that
You shaped our lives
And may each one who breathes

Join with others who breathe
In the delight of shared knowing
That You are the Source of all breath.

Assist us in learning how to partner
With family, neighbors, and friends.
Aid us in dissolving old enmities.

May we come to honor,
Even in those whom we fear,
Your image and form, Your light
Dwelling in their hearts.

May we soon see the day when
Your House will be indeed
The House of prayer for all peoples,
Named and celebrated
In every tongue and speech.
On that day You will be one
And one with all cosmic Life.

Amen!

Rabbi Zalman Schachter-Shalomi
World Wisdom Chair, The Naropa Institute, Colorado

At last we have come to it.
One small and fragile speck of interstellar dust.
One infinitely tiny cell of cosmic life.
A single jot of total potential waiting to be released.
Like the first bacterium leaping into life,
The Earth stands poised to exhale
The breath of human consciousness
Into the dark and lonely void of space.
A second Genesis
In this other Eden.
After four billion years of evolutionary struggle,
A new synthesis
Of human and universal consciousness.
At last we have come to it.

This is untraveled ground.

Four billion years
For consciousness to emerge,
Then in only forty thousand more
To move from cave to high-rise tower,
From stone tool to robots on the assembly line.
All this, but still stuck in territorial grief,
Remaining deaf to love beyond the tribe,
And soaking the ground with blood in every land.

Now the higher calling struggles to be heard.
For the most part
The din and dance of boom and bust
Still drowns it out,

While the very Earth
Trembles more than a little
Under the burden.

No flash of transformation is pending.
The way of evolution was never thus.
But always in the sheltered margins of the main event,
The questing mutant messengers have formed,
Secured their strength,
And waited for their moment in the light.

13

So will it be again,
As the pressure builds for consciousness
To hear the higher call,
Then reach, transform, and finally transcend.

Unless . . .
Unless the sweep of chance wipes all that out,
Because we did not learn to play the part
Our consciousness created for us,
And like a curious willful child
Without a parent's guiding hand
We fall into the shimmering pond and drown.

So, at last we have come to it.
Whether to fashion a value shift among all cultures
Replacing sense of separation
With understanding of the all,
Or lose our gains against a higher hand.

At last we have come to it.

Desmond Berghofer
The Institute for Ethical Leadership, Canada

Let us invoke our ancestors,
   both spiritual and genetic.
For we are the sole reason for their existence.

Let us invoke the children,
   and their children.
For they are the sole reason for our existence.

Let us invoke the mountains and rivers and this great earth
   and acknowledge our intimacy and co-dependency
with all things sentient and insentient.

Let us reflect that the gift of life
   is more fragile than the dewdrops
on the tips of the morning grasses.

Then, let us vow.
Let us vow to heal and nourish.
Let us vow to love and share.
Let us vow to alleviate suffering and bondage.
Let us vow to manifest peace and joy
   with wisdom and compassion.
May this new century be known to future generations as
   The Great Millennium of the Endless Spring.

John Daido Loori, Roshi
Zen Mountain Monastery, New York

Everywhere the transformation will look different, just as spring comes to each spot with subtly different signs and vestiges. In city and suburb, in poor nation and rich nation, in tropic and farm belt and pole, environmental hope will appear in various disguises. Some places it will come as a sleek new bus or a bike path; in others as a cleaned-up slum, a repaired school, a cry of joy at the birth of a baby girl. Here in the Appalachians, on some not-too-distant day, I will wake up and drink a glass of fresh milk from a neighbor's small dairy; that night I will hear a pack of wolves howling from Buck Hill. And it will raise the hair on my arms, and it will fill me up with hope. Hope that the greenhouse effect might someday abate. Hope that this society might be starting the climb down from overdevelopment. Not hope that everything will be fine—everything isn't going to be fine. But hope that the sky is brightening a little in the East.

15

Bill McKibben
Author, New York

16

The springtime of the
epoch
comes in the tender shoots of
green hope
pushing up through discouragement.
Bitter winds shake
our branches even as our
poignant grace of
blossoms
burst open into joy.

An epoch's spring and
promise

is not without storm and shaking,

but the sunny assurance of daffodils
can hold us steady

till the might of our broad river
is overhung with green
summer
ease.

Nancy-Rose Meeker
Poet, Canada

Visions of Hope

There is a grace approaching
that we shun as much as death.
It is the completion of our birth.

It does not come in time, but in timelessness
when the mind sinks into the heart
and we remember who we are.

It is an insistent grace that draws us
to the edge and beckons us to surrender
safe territory and enter our enormity.

We know we must pass beyond knowing
and fear the shedding.

But we are pulled upward
    nonetheless
through forgotten ghosts
    and unexpected angels
realizing it doesn't make sense
    to make sense anymore

This morning the universe danced before you
as you sang—it loves that song!

Stephen and Ondrea Levine
Teachers and authors, New Mexico

Lord, where shall we find the courage to envisage a new beginning? Out of the depths, Father, Mother, we come to you. In our confusion we cry to you . . . and suddenly comes the exciting news!

You, who abide in heavenly realms, you have come to us! You have not considered the smallness of our planet or the ephemeral nature of our lives. It is grace—pure, unlimited grace! Our human predicament you have made yours, and now you announce a new morning, a new beginning: "And I saw the holy city, the New Jerusalem coming down out of heaven from God. . . . See, I am making all things new" (Revelation 21:2, 5).

The vision of your future shakes out our frustration, opens our eyes to discern your Spirit. Behind the limits of our human expectations, you are at work. A different tomorrow is possible. This faith leads us into the new millennium with hope and anticipation. This vision enlists us, mobilizes us, sends us to work for the future. It is worthwhile to struggle for justice, to work for peace, to announce reconciliation, to anticipate the reality of a world where "they shall beat their swords into plowshares and their spears into pruning hooks. Nation shall not lift up sword against nation, neither shall they learn war any more" (Isaiah 2:4). We go into the future with the expectation of the surprises that the Holy Spirit prepares. We go into the millennium with the assurance, O Father and Mother, that you will be there, waiting for us. In this we trust. Amen.

Rev. Emilio Castro
Former General Secretary,
World Council of Churches, Switzerland

We have entered a new Middle Ages, a time of plague, famine, violence, extreme class disparity, and religious fanaticism—and also (as in the late Middle Ages) a time of profound discovery and change. A time when it is terribly important, and often dangerous, to preserve values and knowledge—to stand up for visions that most of this crazed world can't comprehend or tolerate.

The value of having an inner map of the world as it is (not as it's broadcast) is this: it allows you to know that your task is larger than yourself. If you choose, just by virtue of being a decent person, you are entrusted with passing on something of value through a dark, crazy time—preserving your integrity, in your way, by your acts and your very breathing for those who will build again when this chaos exhausts itself. People who assume the burden of their own integrity are free—because integrity is freedom, and (as Nelson Mandela proved) its force can't be quelled even when a person of integrity is jailed. The future lives in our individual, often lonely, and certainly unprofitable acts of integrity, or it doesn't live at all.

Michael Ventura
Author, California

Dear God,

The world is not as it should be.
There is violence and famine and sickness and pain.
    Let those things die, dear Lord.
May we be reborn.

My heart at times is not as it should be.
There is conflict, unforgiveness, judgment, and rage.
    Let those things die, dear Lord.
May I be reborn.

As we embark upon the newness of the coming age,
may the wickedness which marked the old
be cast away by Love.
    Let wickedness die, dear Lord.
May we be reborn.

Where a brother sees not
the beauty of his brother,
and a sister sees not
the glory of her sister.
Where a brother sees not the innocence of his sister,
and a sister sees not the brilliance of her brother.
May illusions die, dear Lord,
May we be reborn.

Take this millennium,
and all ages past,
and strip them of their lovelessness.
May only love remain.
Forgive the horror,
exalt the glory,

redeem the past,
release the future,
wipe away all tears,
deliver us to joy,
correct our thinking
and heal our hearts.

May fear now die, dear Lord,
may we be no longer who we used to be.
Release Your glory
which lies within us,
that all the world might be reborn.
This is my prayer
for the age upon us.
This is my prayer
for me.

Amen.
May we be reborn.
Amen.

Marianne Williamson
Author and speaker, California

21

22

We pray to make it whole,
tip the world on edge and
follow the trail home, singing.
Our voices carry
into the future,
our brief language
a migration of words,
slow voice of mountain,
wandering voices of caribou, wind,
blown seed, all the
lost languages wandering
through seasons, moon and sun,
wandering through centuries,
drifting, every year
the grasses return, the birds
begin to sing,
the sky clears and
we can see forever.

Gary Lawless
Poet, Maine

That the coming century be a century of life! This has been my prayer; for this I will work until my final moment.

The trend of history is clear: from an era of materialism, to an era of the mind, to a millennium of life—the latter an era in which reverence for life, for its utter dignity and sanctity, is the absolute standard against which other, relative values are judged.

23

Only a new understanding of life—of its infinity and eternity—can serve as the indestructible foundation for an era of happiness for all.

Only a human revolution, a transformation in the depths of each person's life—from suspicion to trust, from hatred to fraternity, from egoism to caring, from powerlessness to real strength—can bring forth a new century of life.

A century of life! Lit by the sparkling smiles, resounding with the pealing laughter of all the world's parents and children!

Daisaku Ikeda
President, Soka Gakkai International, Japan

May we find each other in the silence between the words.
May we heal the loneliness of our expertise with the wisdom
    of our service.
May we honor in ourselves and all others
    the deep and simple impulse to live,
    to find sacred space and open land.
May we remember that the yearning to be holy is a part of
    everyone
    and the only hope for the next thousand years.

Rachel Naomi Remen, M.D.
Author, co-founder,
Commonweal Cancer Help Program, California

*　　*　　*

My prayer for the millennium is a dance, a wild, blissful dance, a paean of beat and bone and breath and blood.

It's a dance driven by spirit, fueled by spirit. It rocks me in the world beat, whipping me into ten thousand shapes. I reel from blue dance to elbow dance to fiery, funky, free dances. Like a prayer wheel, I spin in the winds of time; in the downbeat of the mother, in the dark heart of prayer, I soak in the mystery. And I do this for you and me and everybody we know and those we don't know. It's my offering.

Inside my cathedral of bones, my blood pulses, my skin tingles with sweat—pounding heart, swirling breath—and, for a moment, I remember: God is the dance.

Gabrielle Roth
Author, philosopher, and healer, The Moving Center, New York

Visions of Hope

I pray to the great Spiritual Power in which I live and move and have my being. I pray to God. I pray that we may at all times keep our minds open to new ideas and shun dogma; that we may grow in our understanding of the nature of all living beings and our connectedness with the natural world; that we may become ever more filled with generosity of spirit and true compassion and love for all life; that we may strive to heal the hurts that we have inflicted on nature and control our greed for material things, knowing that our actions are harming our natural world; that we may value each and every human being for who he is, for who she is, reaching to the spirit that is within, knowing the power of each individual to change the world.

I pray that we may learn the peace that comes with forgiving and the strength we gain in loving; that we may learn to take nothing for granted in this life; that we may learn to see and understand with our hearts; that we may learn to join in our being.

I pray for these things with humility; I pray because of the hope that is within me, and because of my faith in the ultimate triumph of the human spirit; I pray because of my love for Creation, and because of my trust in God. I pray, above all, for peace throughout the world.

Jane Goodall
Ethnologist, The Jane Goodall Institute, Maryland

Feeling the weight of duality in either palm, and bringing our palms together in the gesture of prayer, we hold the whole world in our hands and dare to dream:

26

that the world of self
and the world of other
meet and join in the heart
as the lover receives the
   beloved
in union, now, and forever;

that the world of soulful
   darkness
and the world of spiritual
   light
meet and join one another
in union, now, and forever;

that the world of silent repose
and the world of courageous
   action
meet and join one another
in union, now, and forever;

that the world of impregnat-
   ing joy
and the world of fruitful
   sorrow
meet and join one another
in union, now, and forever;

that the world of fluid heart
and the world of formal mind
meet and join one another
in union, now, and forever;

that all of the time past
and all of the time yet to
   come
may meet and join one
   another
in union, now, and forever.
   Amen.

Joseph Jastrab
Counselor, teacher, author, and wilderness guide,
Earthrise Foundation, New York

May Respect crowd out the weed of Violence
and Community spring from the ashes of Isolation.
May the stories of our grandmothers and grandfathers
once again nourish the growing souls of our children.

May we see the Divine in one another and in nature
that the Earth may be healed and all her children
have an abundance of food, freedom, and loving-kindness
as we give willingly and with heartfelt joy to one another.

27

May the music of shared laughter replace cries of suffering
as the Great Tree of Peace takes root in every heart.
May we offer a renewed and resurrected World
to the Creator with infinite gratitude and thanksgiving.

Joan Zakon Borysenko
Author and speaker, Colorado

On the way home
all the restaurants will serve miso soup

On the way home
exotic notebook stores will blossom in small towns in Nevada

On the way home
Utah will be festooned w/ mirth
Mormons will be dancing in the streets in gauzy chatchkas

One the way home
Everyone will leave the casinos and the
slot machines and go outside
to stare at the beauty of the mountains, of the sky, of each
     other

On the way home
All the boys & girls in the secret desert bordellos
will have set up temples of free love festooned with mimosa
they will teach karma-mudra to joyful redneck ranchers
who have set all their cows free and now drink only amrita

On the way home
every cafe in Wyoming will be holding a potlatch
poverty will thus be abolished

On the way home
everyone we meet will try to read us a poem
invite us in for a story there being no news
but what travelers bring, all TV having died

On the way home
it will be easy to find pure water, organic tomatoes, friendly
     conversation

Visions of Hope

We'll give & receive delightful music & blessings at every gas
    station
(all the gas will be free)

On the way home
all the truck drivers will drive politely
the traveling summer tourists will beam at their kids

our old Toyota will love going up mountain passes
openhearted & unsuspicious people & lizards
prairie dogs, wolves, & magpies will sing together & picnic
at sunset beside the road

Everyone will get where they're going
Everyone will be peaceful
Everyone will like it when they get there

All obstacles smoothed
auspiciousness & pleasure
will sit like a raven dakini
on every roof.

Diane di Prima
"A Prayer for the Road"
Poet, California

May we give birth to a new Dream of the People.
A dream that can sustain us in the new millennium.
A dream that remembers that there is no separation
       between spirit and matter.
A dream that infuses the life of the people
       with the power of the erotic.
A dream that reminds us of what is holy.

I call on a dream that remembers
       the power of life-giving moisture
that recognizes the smell of the sea
       where it caresses the shore
in the scent of our sweat
in the salt of our tears
in the slippery wetness that pours
from between the soft thighs
of a woman well loved.

I call on a dream that reminds us
to focus on our fingertips,
on the shape and weight of our hand
on blood and bone and a thousand nerve endings
as we raise an apple
       to our mouths
       and let the tip of our tongues
       slide on the round, smooth firmness
       of the cool surface
and feel the spray of juice
as our teeth pierce the skin
and enter the softness
       inside.

A dream that helps us taste
the weeks of rain and sun
the ripening on the tree
the labor of the farmer
        touch of the fruit-picker
        journey of the men and women
        who bring fruits
        from grove to table.
I call on a Dream of the People that remembers
        there is no separation
that knows
        each act lived fully awake
        cannot help but be
both prayer and lovemaking.

Oriah Mountain Dreamer
Author and teacher, Canada

32

The doors of the temple will remain open.
There will be no walls.

The sacred letters will glow
beneath the lights of spheres celestial.

The poor will come to end their thirst
from lakes of wine.

And as we tilt our cups we will see
the reflections of those yet to be born
feeding extinct species by the hand,
humming to dragonflies in copulation.

All sentient beings

in the midst of celebration,
medicine steaming within our veins,
butter dripping forth from the wheat
of our grasp.

Charlie Mehrhoff
Poet, New Mexico

Ho Two-Legged!
Behold . . .
Keep trying, have hope!
Wherever, upon our planet.

Tribes of Two-Legged existed.
Wa nah, they co-existed with all things.
Winged, finned, four-legged, and the planted ones.
Streams, brooks ran clear and the wind was clean.

The knowledge is still here!
A Great Way indeed.
Their lifestyle protected Ina Makah, Mother Earth.
Day upon day, century following century.

Ho Two-Legged!
Total Communication and shared knowledge is here . . . Now!
It can . . . all return!
Because . . . *Mitakuye Oyasin;* we are all related!

Ed McGaa, Eagle Man
Oglala Sioux, Minnesota

Visions of Hope

34

I think of my motherland, Cambodia, like an invocation I'd give to the world, dreaming that by the year 2000, peace will truly come to this wounded nation of mass genocide and violence.

I think of her becoming a land of gardens, a rain forest of air and life, a country of forgiveness and compassion. She will represent understanding beyond borders and become a peace-maker of neighboring conflicts with the Vietnamese, the Thais, and ourselves.

All her children will have a childhood, a generation with both parents alive and siblings to play with. No child will be forced to hold a gun for someone else's political or economic greed.

All the land mines will have been destroyed from the land her people farm to eat. All land mines banned from the world.

There will be playgrounds instead of war zones.
There will be more schools instead of brothels and nightclubs.
The children will sing songs of joy instead of terror.
They will learn how to read love instead of hate.
And each child will have enough to eat and clean water to
    drink.

My homeland will be green again—she will sprout seeds of peace into spring blossoms of love and joy. Her tropical trees will be left unlogged. Her abundant fruit shared. Her forests an earthly paradise. She will be serene, beautiful, and full of charms like the statues carved on her temple walls, filled with peace and hiding smiles. Her people will have been made strong and wise from all the suffering they have endured.

Visions of Hope

The bigger and more wealthy countries will stop selling her arms to kill her own people. They will become good role models for her political and spiritual development. They will respect her as an equal and love her as their own sister.

Those nations with skills to share, friendship to gain, and love to give will sincerely come to help her, give her encouragement, and provide her with the support needed to keep her people growing trees instead of cutting them down to pay their debt.

35

I think of Cambodia as one nation loved, one nation healed and freed from war and hate. Imagine the earth with all nations loved and treated when sick or diseased. Imagine families of people willing to share, to understand and learn from each other. Imagine all the wisdom and the experiences that we could gather to make our planet one home and ourselves one people, united in our diversity. Imagine—

Chath Piersath
Habitat for Humanity International, Cambodia

36

The Buddha got enlightened
Under a tree

Saw the morning star

And touched the earth
As witness

In the next millennium
Which is right now

All of us
Will recognize
We too
Are Buddhas

And will
Plant more trees
Deep in the earth

Under which more Buddhas
Will sit

And plant more trees
Under which

Forever and ever
More.

Rick Fields
Author and editor, California

These are the ways a world ends:

The Tibetan—the Kali Yuga marked by the tyranny of materialism while bearers of sacred teachings are persecuted;
The Manacean—eternal spiritual warfare as snake devours tail;

The Aztec—the return of the Iron Age reigned by Prince of Darkness, Lord of the Smoking Mirror;
The Incan—the tools of humans rise up to destroy the earth;
The Hopi—Koyaanisqatsi and life swirling further out of balance;
The Technosapien—Y2K Bug scrambles our languages back to Babel;
The Arapahoe—consumed by water in another Great Flood;
The Mayan—the year 2012 A.D. Cataclysm;
The Roman—Death by over-entertainment;
The Greek—Pandemonium;
The Islamic—Jihad;
The Christian—Armageddon, the Four Horsemen of the Apocalypse trample the deviant and heretic masses;
The American—"Not with a bang but a whimper."

Amid such ill foreboding
and mad daily crossfire,
Hear the choir
of courageous angels sing:

"We shall overcome. We shall overcome. We shall overcome some day."

Joseph Richey
Poet and editor, Colorado

38

To live at this moment when a new possibility opens for a millennium of contentment, tranquility, and peace is a rare opportunity. In silence I am mindful how the life breath passes through my nostrils and reaches every one of my cells, bringing tranquility to both my mind and my body. The air I breathe in and breathe out has been enriched and shared by all living beings; so the whole of humanity, the animal kingdom, and the plant kingdom are related to me. May the energies of my loving-kindness reach out to all of them and make them well and happy. May such thoughts and feelings radiated by everyone form and create loving-kindness that will make our minds and hearts open up for the good of all.

May this loving-kindness generate compassionate action in and for all human beings and all of nature. Compassionate action eradicates poverty, competition, and violence from our world. May my sisters and brothers and relatives in nature join hands with me to build peace and the highest possible levels of spiritual attainment.

A. T. Ariyaratne
Founder, Sarvodaya Movement, Sri Lanka

There's something remarkable, universally unique about the planetary situation which we are yet to create. Something the Creator couldn't think up except through us.

Seeing what life will be like in the year 3000 is currently beyond our greatest visionaries and futurologists. So we must focus on the critical decades straight ahead. We need to do things we can truly respect ourselves for. We need to treat others as we would have them treat us—in our billions.

The whole universe is watching. They're waiting to see us pull off the Big One! Mission Impossible, yet entirely achievable. They're fascinated at the straits we have gotten into. No one but us could have thought up today's global situation. It's wonderful, unique, intensely meaningful. This is the place to be.

In this light, my prayer for the new millennium is this: May we see, love, and create the simple, the human, and the natural.

All else will emerge. Despite much evidence to the contrary in the twentieth century, I feel quietly, optimistically confident that this prayer will be answered in the twenty-first. Is there any choice?

Palden Jenkins
Author, editor, and teacher, England

Come be our mother   we are your young ones
Come be our bride   we are your lover
Come be our dwelling   we are your inhabitants
Come be our game   we are your players
Come be our punishment   we are your sinners
Come be our ocean   we are your swimmers
Come be our victory   we are your army
Come be our laughter   we are your story
Come be our Shekhinah   we are your glory
We believe that you live
Though you delay   we believe you will certainly come

When the transformation happens as it must
When we remember
When she wakes from her long repose in us
When she wipes the nightmare
Of history from her eyes
When she returns from exile
When she utters her voice in the streets
In the opening of the gates
When she enters the modern world
When she crosses the land
Shaking her breasts and hips
With timbrels and with dances
Magnified and sanctified
Exalted and honored
Blessed and glorified
When she causes tyranny
To vanish
When she and he meet
When they behold each other face to face

Visions of Hope

When they become naked and not ashamed
On that day will our God be One
And their name One

Shekhinah bless us and keep us
Shekhinah shine your face on us
Shekhinah turn your countenance
To us and give us peace

Alicia Ostriker
"A Prayer to the Shekhinah"
Author and professor of English,
Rutgers University, New Jersey

* * *

Professing unshakable reliance upon you our God, and human reliance upon one another, we, women and men of your creation, joined in love, open wide the window of a new time in which the sun will refresh equally the rich and the poor, the animals of the sea and the birds of the air, the plants of the earth and the stones of the ages—indeed, all creation.

May our trust in your providence and in each other lead us to act justly, to love tenderly, to walk humbly, and to live together in peace on this earth. Amen

Sr. Mary Ann Coyle, S.L.
Sisters of Loretto, Colorado

There dwells within the Source that at every moment brings us forth in creative love, brings us forth in the Divine Image, each of us, to be more beautiful than Michelangelo's *David*, more serene than the Buddha, more joyful than the Dalai Lama, more loving than Mother Teresa, a unique image of the Image, to bring to this small world of ours our own particular ray of healing light.

42

Together we can create a new millennium, healed of all the wounds of the passing one, as we each allow ourselves to be recreated in the fullness and be that freely given gift to each other.

Let us not be held captive to a narrow theology of scarcity but open to the flood of the Divine Generosity; let it pour out through us, embracing every woman and man, every particle of this wondrous creation that is our common heritage, responsibility, and glory.

Br. M. Basil Pennington, O.C.S.O.
Cistercian Spencer, monk, St. Joseph's Abbey, Massachusetts

A man makes his prayers; he sings his songs. He considers all that is important and special to him—his home, his children, his language, the self that he is. He must make spiritual and physical preparation before anything else. Only then does anything begin.

A man leaves; he encounters all manner of things. He has adventures, meets people, acquires knowledge; goes different places; he is always looking. Sometimes the traveling is hazardous; sometimes he finds meaning and sometimes he is destitute. But he continues; he must. His traveling is a prayer as well, and he must keep on.

A man returns, and even the returning has moments of despair and tragedy. But there is beauty and there is joy. At times he is confused, and at times he sees with utter clarity. It is all part of the traveling that is a prayer. There are things he must go through before he can bring back what he seeks, before he can return to himself.

The rain comes and falls. The *shiwana* have heeded the man, and they have come. The man has brought back the rain. It falls, and it is nourishing. The man returns to the strength that his selfhood is, his home, his people, his language, the knowledge of who he is. The cycle has been traveled; life has beauty and meaning, and it will continue because life has no end.

Simon J. Ortiz
Author, Acoma Pueblo, New Mexico

44

One day you finally knew
what you had to do, and began,
though the voices around you
kept shouting
their bad advice—
though the whole house
began to tremble
and you felt the old tug
at your ankles.
"Mend my life!"
each voice cried.
But you didn't stop.
You knew what you had to do,
though the wind pried
with its stiff fingers
at the very foundations—
though their melancholy
was terrible.
It was already late
enough, and a wild night,
and the road full of fallen
branches and stones.
But little by little,
as you left their voices behind,
the stars began to burn
through the sheets of clouds,
and there was a new voice,
which you slowly
recognized as your own,

Visions of Hope

that kept you company
as you strode deeper and deeper
into the world,
determined to do
the only thing you could do—
determined to save
the only life you could save.

Mary Oliver
Poet, Massachusetts and Vermont

45

Part 2

OPENING
OUR HEARTS

God will not change the condition of a people
until they change what is in their hearts.

KORAN 13:11

The prayers in Part 2 are like prayer beads for our hearts. They offer simple, generous counsel: love, listen, be open to the unknown, and do not turn away from suffering. They show us how to prepare ourselves, to be present and compassionate.

> Open your fists
> into embraces
> Open your arms' length
> into loving circles.
> *James Broughton*

Many people look to their political leaders to take care of things for them, and they criticize those leaders for their failures. Yet if the many contributors to this book share one common denominator it is their belief that social change is rooted in the personal practice of love. How often have we seen the truth of the adage "When the people lead, the leaders will follow"? Transformative change in a society begins with a change of heart within its people. Opening our hearts to the beauty and pain of the world, allowing these to be held in us without sentimentality, anger, or denial, in itself is a powerful gift to the future. It is an act of love that creates a field of loving-kindness.

The subject of love is inexhaustible. In that little word is hidden the key to our own happiness as well as to the survival of the world. While modern culture has generated oceans of information, we are rarely the wiser for it. Information is not our greatest need; opening our hearts to the creative and life-giving spirit of love *is*.

As the twentieth century concludes with the "nanosecond nineties," our lives are frenzied with fast food, fast banking, fast funerals, sound-bite news, and instant analysis. Success is measured by speed, and speed annihilates the spaciousness of the moment. A number of the prayers here speak to this theme, reminding us to slow down, breathe, and attend.

> The Lord is my pace-setter, I shall not rush.
> He makes me stop and rest for quiet intervals . . .
> *The Nuns' Twenty-Third Psalm*

We might see the turning of the millennium, and all such anniversaries, as a special gift of time—a reminder that time is quality, not simply quantity. As we pause, breathe, and attend to the moment, life reveals its timeless abundance and promise. This is the practice of *opening*. Through it we recover the spaciousness and generosity that are our birthright.

Opening our hearts also makes us vulnerable. In that vulnerability we fear that they may be broken. And yes, the world's pain does break our hearts, over and over again. But a broken heart is not a paralyzed one. Buddha, Jesus, Muhammad, and the saints, prophets, and masters of all religions have revealed this. Hearts are broken *open,* not destroyed; and from an open heart's capacity to be with suffering, healing arises. Healing is not something that can be offered from a distance, an outside attempt to "fix" a problem. Rather, healing emerges from the act of "being with" suffering. The healing relationship is established by the authentic presence of an open heart.

51

In the name of the daybreak
and the eyelids of morning
and the wayfaring moon
and the night when it departs,

I swear I will not dishonor
my soul with hatred,
but offer myself humbly
as a guardian of nature,
as a healer of misery,
as a messenger of wonder,
as an architect of peace.

In the name of the sun and its mirrors
and the day that embraces it
and the cloud veils drawn over it
and the uttermost night
and the male and the female
and the plants bursting with seed
and the crowning seasons
of the firefly and the apple,

I will honor all life—
wherever and in whatever form
it may dwell—on Earth my home,
and in the mansions of the stars.

Diane Ackerman
Author, New York

The thing is
to love life
to love it even when you have no
stomach for it, when everything you've held
dear crumbles like burnt paper in your hands
and your throat is filled with the silt of it.
When grief sits with you so heavily
it's like heat, tropical, moist
thickening the air so it's heavy like water
more fit for gills than lungs.
When grief weights you like your own flesh
only more of it, an obesity of grief.
How long can a body withstand this? you think,
and yet you hold life like a face between your palms,
a plain face, with no charming smile
or twinkle in her eye,
and you say, yes, I will take you
I will love you, again.

53

Ellen Bass
Author, California

Let us understand
The gravity of our situation.

Let us understand
That our only redemption
Is love.

Love for a small, endangered planet
On which we are utterly dependent.

Only love can transform us
From plunderers and savagers
Into Earthkeepers and peacemakers.

Only love can show us
The integrity and rights
Of all other beings.

Only love can open our eyes
To the truth and beauty
That surround us.

Only love can teach us
The humility we need
To live on this Earth.

And only love can now save us
From extinction.

Mary de La Valette
Poet and activist,
Gaia Institute, Massachusetts

We look with uncertainty
Beyond the old choices for
Clear-cut answers
to a softer, more permeable aliveness
Which is every moment
At the brink of death;
For something new is being born in us
If we but let it.
We stand at a new doorway,
Awaiting that which comes . . .
Daring to be human creatures.
Vulnerable to the beauty of existence.
Learning to love.

55

Anne Hillman
Author and international
lecturer, California

*   *   *

I pray for deep listening in the new century—listening
alone—listening together—listening to others—listening to
oneself—listening to the earth—listening to the universe—
listening to the abundance that is—awakening to and feeling
sound and silence as all there is—helping to create an atmosphere of opening for all to be heard, with the understanding that listening is healing. Deep listening in all its
variations is infinite. Deep listening is love.

Pauline Oliveros
Composer, New York

Is this love that rushes towards the rim to meet you
A main thread in the inwardness of things?
Without it would the great externality loosen and unravel?
Is it our purpose to see and say that the world is good?
And could we have seen this and said it, beloved,
While you seemed indubitable?
I do not know.

I stand with hands dangling empty at my sides.
I have no wisdom bequeathed to me by ancestors.
The stars are equivocal, and around me
Nature is in sorest travail, weeping.

I love you.

This is the only sacred word in my keeping.
This is the last trace,
The last print in our hearts' waste,
Of the migration of a thousand traditions,
A thousand embodiments of wisdom.
I stand with useless hands,
And out of the transparency of my poverty,
I offer you this, my single gift.

Freya Mathews
Professor of Philosophy, La Trobe University, Australia

I have been convoked by Love!
    The true one that creates, awaits, and discovers
    because it is stronger than death.

The one that reaches us from the other side of the zenith
    and submerges itself in the depths of the nadir.

57

The one that extends my arms toward the infinite
And invites me to embrace the cosmos with its tenderness.
The one that opens my eyes to the mystery that I am
In the unfathomable depth of your eyes
And that bestows on me one step at
    a time victory over fear,
Surely taking me
to the abundant fountain of life.
I have been invited to Love,
Whose waves shake
My small clay pot vibrantly
Yes! It comes from Him.
And toward Him I am carried.

My entire being gives itself over
Ecstatically to His embrace
Into the very heart
Of beatitude.

Julia Esquivel
Author, Mayan Indian, Guatemala

May I, may you, may we
not die unlived lives.
May none of us live in fear
of falling or catching fire.
May we choose to inhabit our days,
to allow our living to open us,
to make us less afraid,
more accessible,
to loosen our hearts
until they become wings,
torches, promises.
May each of us choose to risk our significance;
to live so that which comes to us as seed
goes to the next as blossom
and that which comes to us as blossom,
goes on as fruit.

Dawna Markova
Author and editor, Utah

Rain fell today
and somewhere lotus flowers are blossoming.
So are we.
Defying the impossible
    in the shelter and warmth of each other's hearts,
extending the night, caressing the stars,
And knowing each other's hearts
    is our human bliss.

Jarvis Jay Masters
Death Row, San Quentin

*   *   *

My simple prayer is that in all things I learn to love well.
That I learn to touch the ever-changing seasons of life
    with a great heart of compassion.
That I live with the peace and justice I wish for the earth.
That I learn to care fully and let go gracefully.
That I enjoy the abundance of the earth and return to it
    from the natural generosity that is our human birthright.
That through my own life, through joy and sorrow
    in thought, word, and deed,
I bring benefit and blessings to all that lives.
That my heart and the hearts of all beings learn to be free.

Jack Kornfield
Buddhist meditation teacher, Spirit Rock Center, California

Opening Our Hearts

Thank you God for who I am.
Thank you for You,
for all living beings,
for the love I feel that makes me live
every moment of my life with great joy,
helping me bring joy
to all that my life touches.

Thank you God for the opportunities I have every day
to express the best I have in me,
for being able to be of service to every person I meet.

Thank you God for the perfect peace I feel inside,
tranquility, serenity, Divine Quietness.
Thank you for everything I learn
from all I experience and all I create every day.

Thank you God for inspiring me,
for helping me create Heaven on Earth
now, and now, and now,
and in every moment I think, speak, and act.

Thank you God
for being who I am.
Thank you,
thank you,
thank you.

Oscar Motomura
Director, AMANA-KEY, *Brazil*

The world is fast losing its soul
but you don't have to surrender yours.
You don't have to live on a mechanical globe.
You don't have to tame your deep-forest passions.
You don't have to suppress your radiant beauty.

Live your joy,
Go against the grain.
Don't be made timid by worried rejection.
Let nature's curious wisdom fill you.
Let the world's mystical heritage guide you.
Paint your canvases,
play your tunes.

Give your all to the words that are born from you.
Your father and your father's heaven
will never abandon you
but always love
the scintilla of your spirit.

Thomas Moore
Author, New Hampshire

62

My Lord, supreme being of this universe,
let my lips sing the praise of the goodness surrounding me
not affected by the evil that is so rampant,
let my heart glow with the love for them who show affection
    for me,
and acceptance for others who do not.

Give me the strength to continue that which I do best,
that I may add an iota to the transformation of this planet,
let me have the spark to ignite others in joining me,
the wisdom to choose the causes that I should support,
that I may join others in the effort to make this earth a better
    place to live,
my grain of sand being one in the new edifice,
that I could say at the end of the day
that I was all that I could be for my dear ones,
for others not as fortunate as I have been,
and for this planet,
being here for much more than just myself,
even when it was not always easy.

Tsvi Meidav
Geothermal energy developer, California

Spiritual awakening is frequently described as a journey to the top of a mountain. We leave our attachments and our worldliness behind and slowly make our way to the top. At the peak we have transcended all pain. The only problem with this metaphor is that we leave all the others behind—our drunken brother, our schizophrenic sister, our tormented animals and friends. Their suffering continues, unrelieved by our personal escape.

In the process of discovering our true nature, the journey goes down, not up. It's as if the mountain pointed toward the center of the earth instead of reaching into the sky. Instead of transcending the suffering of all creatures, we move toward the turbulence and doubt. We jump into it. We slide into it. We tiptoe into it. We move toward it however we can. We explore the reality and unpredictability of insecurity and pain, and we try not to push it away. If it takes years, if it takes lifetimes, we will let it be as it is. At our own pace, without speed or aggression, we move down and down and down. With us move millions of others, our companions in awakening from fear. At the bottom we discover water, the healing water of compassion. Right down there in the thick of things, we discover the love that will not die.

Bhiksuni Pema Chodron
Buddhist teacher and abbess, Gampo Abbey, Canada

God of mercy and love,
at the dawn of the new millennium my heart and mind to you
    I turn
in loving gratitude, in joyful praise and in humble adoration
for the gift of Jesus, your Son, you sent to me,
for the spirit of life you instilled in me,
for the gift of love I receive and give,
for the brothers and sisters all over the world,
for the black and the white, for the old and the young, for the
    rich and the poor,
for the joys and the sorrows that enrich my life,
for the whole of creation, a precious gift to cherish and love.

O my God, loving and compassionate,
at the dawn of the new millennium
open my heart and the hearts of all to the new dimensions of
    the coming era.

Open my heart, O Lord, to a new dimension
of prayer and faith, of love and peace,
of reconciliation and universal brotherhood,
of joyful forgiveness for the wounds, great and small,
past and present, inflicted and received,
of loving respect for the whole of creation.

Lord, God of mercy and love,
may I dare to ask you as my brother Francis did —
make me an instrument of your peace!

Br. Maximilian Mizzi O.F.M. Conv.
The International Franciscan Center for Dialogue, Assisi

I awoke to the confusion of a new day,

The scraps of dreams, memories of yesterday, and new
  cravings creeping into awareness,

The sun spilling its light over all but the shadows and a
  cacophony of sound

From outside and in.

What to make order of? What to let go?

And who makes the choice?

I think I will go down to the river and just watch it flow,

It's been a long time since I have done something really
  important.

David Sluyter
Fetzer Institute, Michigan

I can't decide whether it's my socks
That go on first, or my pants, indecision
On the edge of my bed. Should I brush my teeth, then shave,
Or shave first, then rinse my mouth of a night's swollen journey?
I know that my eyes must first open to be awake,
And each clumsy step toward the kitchen
Leads me to the same bowl and coffee cup.
I look ahead. The boarded-up century sweeps the dust
Of previous minutes, my time on earth.
God, savior in a bright robe, tell us what to do,
Provide order, make it simple as sock or pants,
As certain as the old face I see in morning's new mirror.

Gary Soto
Author, California

Take time to listen to the birds,
            the waves,
            the wind.

Take time to breathe in the air,
            the earth,
            the ocean.

Take time to be still,
      to be silent,
      to allow God to fill you up
      with deep peace and love.

Mairead Maguire
Recipient, Nobel Peace Prize,
Community of the Peace People, Ireland

68

Get articulate.
Move the blood.
Attend periphery.
Prepare to dance the Open Dance.
Learn to gather momentum and
Throw it away.
Explode into the ordinary and
Keep your eyes wide.
Embrace fear.
Suspend doubt.
Specify.
Simplify.
Strengthen.
Launch.
Float.
Dignify the confusion.
Visualize the next step.
Stick your toe in.
Get all wet!

Barbara Dilley
Dancer and teacher, Colorado

The Lord is my pace-setter, I shall not rush.
He makes me stop and rest for quiet intervals,
He provides me with images of stillness, which restore my
    serenity.
He leads me in ways of efficiency through calmness of mind.
And His guidance is peace.
Even though I have a great many things to accomplish each
    day,
I will not fret, for His presence is here.
His timelessness, his all-importance will keep me in balance.
He prepares refreshment and renewal in the midst of my
    activity
By anointing my mind with His oils of tranquility.
My cup of joyous energy overflows.
Surely harmony and effectiveness shall be the fruit of my
    hours, for
I shall walk in the place of my Lord and dwell in His House
    forever.

The Nuns' Twenty-Third Psalm
All Saints Convent, Maryland

We slow to the world,
take a deep breath,
another,
and yet another.
We allow our spiritual gravity to bring us to rest
and find our place.
Remembering bubbles up.
We know this place.

> Here
> we listen to our children,
> laugh from the bottom of our belly,
> heal and are healed by our neighbors,
> touch the ones we love.
> We recognize delight.

In being restored we remember
No effort is complete without the essential ingredient of
    sacred rest.

Wayne Muller
Author and teacher, Bread for the Journey, California

It is difficult to imagine that we could be so loved. And yet in God's eyes we have always been perfect. As a mother loves her child even before conception, merely in desiring her child, we too are truly loved. This force, which I now call God, unites an ovum and sperm, and as the embryo grows, divides its cells in such absolute perfection that a finger appears on the hand and two eyes on the face. How is it possible that each cell knows what its shape and placement should be? This is not a miracle; it's a natural phenomenon.

As we evolve, with our needs and technologies, facing our humanity with its various challenges, its gains and losses, we begin to walk alone, using only our human strength to confront and solve problems. What has become of the connection to that miraculous force that first divided our cells? For each, our task is to re-member: to reestablish and reclaim that which is already true. We are loved, and we have always been loved. It is not a question of merit or accomplishment. The Divine Love is here. We need only unclench our fists and open to It.

Jeanette Berson
Artist and poet, California

Each day I recommit myself
to the almighty power of universal love
and the evolutionary life force of which I am a small part.
I will always be guided by this source of my eternal being
and will walk in faith and hope for life on this earth
and always seek those who share this knowing
as my companions in love and light.
I balance my energy in joy
and in serving my highest purpose—
my universal self.

Hazel Henderson
Economist and author, Florida

72

Forsake your devotion
to predicament and discord
Break the tradition
of rivalry and curse

Quick while there's time
Uproot hostility
Claim your humanity
Insist on brotherhood

73

Open your fists
into embraces
Open your arms' length
into loving circles

Remove every roadblock
to the peaceable kingdom
Outnumber the hawks
Outdistance the angels.

James Broughton
Poet, Washington State

I am praying with my body
>   life speeds up in a frenzy of email and phone messages
>   breathe, slow down, sit
>   Walking along the Front Range breathing in
>   ponderosa pine bark vanilla

I am praying with my speech
>   speaking real experience
>   breaking the chains of
>   money, time, things
>   Speaking words with power to heal

I am praying with my mind
>   remembering the power of intent, caring
>   light and heart pour out over the Great Plains
>   spilling in all directions
>   praying

I am praying with my hands
>   holding your hand I remember
>   this is a gift of love from the heart of the universe
>   every moment precious

I am praying with my heart
>   holding you dear
>   you who are my mother, brother, sister, father
>   like this we can balance the world.

Anne Parker
Professor of Environmental Studies,
The Naropa Institute, Colorado

Albert Einstein was most precise: "Three great powers rule the world," he said, "stupidity, fear, and greed."

How to interrupt this vicious circle? What tool shall we use, and where shall we insert it?

For me the Dalai Lama has marked the way: "My religion," he said once, "is very simple. My religion is kindness."

75

Kindness trumps greed: it asks for sharing. Kindness trumps fear: it calls forth gratefulness and love. Kindness trumps even stupidity, for with sharing and love, one learns.

Kindness is not on political agendas. Kindness is not on financial agendas. Kindness is not on scientific agendas. Kindness is not on technological agendas. Why not? It's inexpensive, simply understood, and universally approved.

The twenty-first century must feature kindness—to the earth and all its species—or there will be little hope for a twenty-second.

Marc Estrin
Author, Vermont

Creator of the Universe
preserve us from our own presumption.
Do not let us close ourselves into ourselves
but open us continually into You.

Let us be more in love with You
than with our notions of You.
Let us stop claiming to know everything
so that we may understand something.

Increase in us kindness.
Make us people who care
and who take care,
who venerate the truth
and recognize each other.

Draw us with an irresistible beauty!

Rabia Terri Harris
Coordinator, Muslim Peace Fellowship, New York

Wakan Tanka, Great Mystery, I, Akicita Wakan Mani, come to you as a small weak human—I ask you to please hear me, for I seek your gifts so that I may know the gifts in others.

I struggle on my journey, Wakan Tanka, my journey is a spiritual war. It takes place inside me as I seek to bring in unison my heart and mind. I wear my hair in braids to signify this pathway.

Wakan Tanka, please grant me the indomitable spirit to continue to clear my mind of my judgments and grievances of others who are different from me. It is what I carry of my early years that taints my vision today. I am motivated by fear and I ask for the strength to talk honestly and compassionately to all my fellow human beings. Without these two virtues, cruelty can arise.

O Wakan Tanka, help me be ready for this new millennium by letting me continue to clear my own heart and mind and let me walk this road of life in the good way, and to walk the talk of you. I pray for the inner peace of humankind and for mother earth to be honored with harmonious life upon her. Hear my prayer, Wakan Tanka.

Mitakuye Oyasin.

We are all related.

Jim LaVallee, Akicita Wakan Mani
Ojibway-Sioux, Canada

My Creator, I am Chitcus, of the Karuk people from the Upper Klamath River near Sumas Bar, California. I stand before you with burning *kishwouf*, Indian medicine. As a Karuk Indian Medicine Man I seek the vision and spiritual guidance to make all things whole as a healer.

My Creator, give me the time-tested wisdom of the Ancient Ones. Grant me the inner strength to bless the four-legged, the winged ones, the two-legged, and the finned ones.

My Creator, as I journey to the Center of the Earth, grant me the strength as I fast, to travel the sacred fire trails; make the medicine fire strong, so that the blessings of the Karuk World Renewal ceremonies at the dark of the moon in August and September are sacred and accepted.

It is this journey I seek which will bless all, to heal all, that which is sacred. Life, my Creator, make the seed of Life whole, make the journey of the four directions true. May the eyes of the eagle soar; may the spirit of the wolf return; may the path we choose be blessed.

May our roots seek others so that they may be filled with Life.

May Mother Earth sustain Life; as water flows, so does Life within us. May it always be pure.

My Creator, as I walk the path of the Ancient Ones, may I be true to the Spirit of Life.

Chitcus
Karuk Indian Medicine Man, California

O Great Spirit . . .
Roll away from me the weight
      of dead and frozen thoughts.
Clear away from me the fogs
      of falsely sweet illusions.
Ignite in my heart
      the warmth of true love
That with new eyes of new love
And my angel at my back
I may see the Truth of the World.
I may feel the Beauty of the World.
And I may act with courage for the good.
O Great Spirit . . .

David Tresemer
Psychologist and playwright, Colorado

Be still and know that I am with you,
says the Lord.
Be still and know I am you,
says the Tao.

We are part of nature and nature is part of us.
We are held by the Hand of God
and we are the Hands of God.

Do not try to live as if you are separate.
You are not.
You are of God,
part of the Tao.
You are within the landscape.
You are elements of the seasons.
You are of both heaven and earth.

Be known for what you are, and make your actions harbingers
    of a better future.
Flow like water round obstacles.
Do not batter your head against a brick wall.
Flow under it and when it collapses,
you will be long gone.

Hold true to God
rest in the Tao,
and you will be carried to where the future needs you.

Martin Palmer
International Consultancy on
Religion, Education, and Culture, England

I pray for the strength to accept
   that lives most often end in tragedy,
      that quests don't always work,
         that understanding is a long and lonely hunt,
      that I can't reason my way to love,
         eat gold,
            or live forever.
               And that none of this matters.

I pray to understand that I am here to find my way back to God, whatever that takes, and all the rest save love and duty is an illusion.

John Taylor Gatto
Educator and author, New York

I am waiting for instructions.

From the sky comes the scope of my unlimited possibility
From the trees comes the calendar of time, ring by ring
From the wind comes the passion that fills me just before I learn
From the water comes my gratitude, for in it I recognize myself.

From paintings on the stone and drums on the mountain I am reminded that I am not the first. From the inquisitive and demanding nature of my niece I am reminded I am not the last.

From the girl child in the sweat shop whose little fingers bring in ten cents an hour, to the poet who shakes the world round when she speaks "Good morning," to the woman beaten beyond recognition by the man who says he loves her, to the activist who wraps herself around a tree as the blades drown out the sound of her beating heart, to the teenager holding the doll she never had after it comes through her body and will be with her for the rest of her life—to all these I cry out my womanness.

From the lovers hiding to the lovers who kiss in the moonlight as bombs fall just yards from their dreams, reminding me to feel joy when athlete and disabled dare to kiss, when Jew and Arab dare to kiss, when Irish and English dare to kiss, when man and man dare to kiss, when woman and woman dare to kiss, when black and white dare to kiss, reminding us all that for as long as loving evokes fear in our hearts, we have yet another mile to walk to heaven.

From the motion of people, movements in search of higher places, at first the object of disapproval and fear, we grow like dancers hurling through space, our blood splattering in the air and floating down in slow motion, the stardust of perfect intention, like skaters holding each other up for the world to see, crashing on brutal ice at essential moments. I am inspired by my peers as we reach to understand our purpose here.

83

I have torn open my soul, worked to a sweat, wept with humiliation, struggled with confusion, battled with apathy and disillusion, confronted my beliefs again and again until I thought I would drown in sorrow; and yet, here I am, on the dawn of a new millennium, profoundly informed by all life and love. I am ready to take the next step. Yet this time, I am filled with calm and grace, I feel less fear than ever before, I have learned compassion in spite of myself, I *do* talk to the trees and listen to the wind, and I am waiting for instructions.

Holly Near
Singer and songwriter, California

84

At a certain point you say to the woods, to the sea, to the mountains, the world, Now I am ready. Now I will stop and be wholly attentive. You empty yourself and wait, listening. After a time you hear it: there is nothing there. There is nothing but those things only, those created objects, discrete, growing or holding, or swaying, being rained on or raining, held, flooding or ebbing, standing, or spread. You feel the world's word as a tension, a hum, a single chorused note everywhere the same. This is it: this hum is the silence. . . .

The silence is all there is. It is the alpha and the omega. It is God's brooding over the face of the waters; it is the blended note of the ten thousand things, the whine of wings. You take a step in the right direction to pray to this silence, and even to address the prayer to "World." Distinctions blur. Quit your tents. Pray without ceasing.

Annie Dillard
Author, Connecticut

Part 3

THIS MOMENT
in TIME

On the same spot I sit today
Others came, in ages past, to sit.
One thousand years, still others will come.
Who is the singer, and who is the listener?
NGUYEN CONG TRU

In our short history, the human species has produced hundreds of systems for measuring time. The Hindus, Chinese, Japanese, Sumerians, Jews, Greeks, Romans, Christians, Muslims, and Africans created a succession of calendars, many of them still in use. With this in mind we must acknowledge the relative nature of all calendars; one is not more "true" than another. While the calendar of the common era has its origins in the birthdate of Christ, biblical scholars contend that Jesus' actual birth occurred somewhere between three and six years prior to the year that equates with zero. As a consequence, the common era millennium we observe is arbitrary, its value symbolic rather than coincident with an exact number of orbits of the earth around the sun since the birth of Christ.

Of course, for Christians the millennium offers a significant moment to remember Jesus' life and to renew their pledge of loyalty to its meaning. But in our increasingly interfaith and secular world, the millennium has come to signify qualities other than Christ's two-thousandth birthday. In this context the word *millennium* means both a moment—that point in time when the odometer on our calendar shows three zeros—and the nearly incomprehensible span of a thousand years. It

This Moment in Time

is a powerful contrast: one moment and a thousand years of moments. In their scale they are utterly different, but in their essence they are identical. Their essence is *now*. Many of the authors in Part 3 remind us that to live in the present is to experience the true miracle of life. Here and right now is the only chance we have to live, to let what is finished be finished, and to open ourselves to the unknown future with the mindfulness that promises rebirth. We are counseled to become present to *this* moment—present in awareness and love.

Propelled by the fast-forward changes of modern society, we find ourselves tumbling headlong toward this millennium moment, a gateway into unknown territory. What could we possibly say about the next thousand years? And how shall we mark this moment? When it arrives and we raise our glasses to propose a toast, what shall we say?

The human urge to ritualize beginnings and to articulate their meaning can be seen in every culture—baptizing babies, launching ships, marrying lovers, starting baseball games with the national anthem, or saying prayers at dawn. Beginnings present a natural moment to speak of our intentions and wishes, of our gratitude and our kinship and what matters most to us. It is a time to reach our hands across all barriers and offer a blessing.

> Let us put on our shoes, the pin-striped shirt
> the blue suit though it shines from long wear,
> let us light the flares and set off fireworks,
> let the wine and beer flow from our necks to our toes,
> because duly we must celebrate
> this immense number that cost so much time,
> so many years and days in bundles,

This Moment in Time

so many hours, so many millions of minutes,
let us celebrate this inauguration.

Pablo Neruda (from the poem "2000")

The turning of the second millennium C.E. into the third will
be observed by more people than any other anniversary in our
species' history. It is relevant, then, to ask: What does this
event mean to us? What do we very diverse peoples share in
common?

This book is one answer to those questions. And Part 3
speaks of the central core of that answer: *we share this moment.*
Here we meet as sisters and brothers. From this "still point
of the turning world," our gestures to one another do have
meaning, and our communion together is real.

This Moment in Time

Another thousand years has completed its cycle.
Nature has responded to each cycle of time.
How have human beings conformed to the demands of time?
How have human beings enhanced the greatness of this
    planet?
Everything we think, say, and do in our lives has a ripple
    effect on the planet.
We never know what is coming,
    but we do know our actions yield consequences.
And so the millennium is a great new beginning.
A sparkling turning point.
And with each turning point there is greater responsibility,
    as well as fresh, invigorating expectation!
It is an auspicious time to pay homage
    to all those who have sacrificed their lives
    for the upliftment of humanity.
It is a chance to make a vow
    to respect and love one another with kindness.
As we turn another corner in time
    let us support one another in our best efforts.
Let us pray to serve the highest in everyone.

May we offer gratitude to the past.
May we extend a warm welcome to the future.
May we live with wisdom in the present.

Together, may we make this world a better paradise.

Gurudev Siddha Peeth Gurumayi Chidvilasananda
Ganeshpuri, India

Bless us O God
and these thy gifts
of anno Domini
two thousand:

    air wrapping its silky husk around us
    great sweeps of overhead blue
        grasping horizons by the rims
    gold of the sun-flakes, scarlet-birded cedar
        lilacs, cathedrals, blankets, and rain
        orange peel and sandalwood,

porches rocking a million stars
the beach, and a salting of gulls on the air.

    campfires and lonely
    vast acres of mercy

that we are about to receive
from your goodness
    your
    incredible greatness

through God whose millennium
    lasts only a cry
    before it is time for
    the next anno Domini
    three thousand:

Bless us O God
and these thy gifts

Sr. Eileen Haugh, O.S.F.
Tau Center, Minnesota

This Moment in Time

In the final days of the century,
the weight of a thousand years,
the exhaustion of trying to mentally hold
a millennium—makes my profile
a question mark, a bent figure
yet smiling in the face of meaninglessness.

* * *

More people living than have ever died.

* * *

A beach, a park;
at dawn, at dusk;
arms uplift, circle, clasp.

Welcome, we sing.
Welcome, we sing,
and we mark the time.

So continue—two, three, four.
Be brave, neighbor.
Be brave.

Gene Keller
Poet and Unitarian, Texas

Now is the time
To climb up the mountain
And reason against habit.
Now is the time.

Now is the time
To renew the barren soil of nature
Ruined by the winds of tyranny.
Now is the time.

Now is the time
To commence the litany of hope.
Now is the time.

Now is the time
To give me roses, not to keep them
For my grave to come.
Give them to me while my heart beats,
Give them today
While my heart yearns for jubilee.
Now is the time . . .

Mzwakhe Mbuli
Performance artist and activist, South Africa

This Moment in Time

94

Brand new millennium, the year 2000,
Requires us to shape up, don't you think?
Three fine zeros in perfect alignment,
A trinity of sacred emptiness.

Three eggs, graceful and tall,
Standing at attention,
Their delicate curves arching
Around blank slates of infinite potential,
Framing the sweet promise
Of condensed power and possibility,
Silently pulsing beneath the surface.

Stately O's, three abreast,
Issuing their call to forgiveness and right action.
It is time, they seem to say,
In their roundness,
To open your heart
And ransom your spirit.
They hint broadly of Heaven.

We are hungry for betterment,
Primed to dissolve our gummy resentments,
Ready to dismiss the hard thoughts
That hold the lush heart hostage,
And cramp and twist the open hand,
Causing it to withdraw.

Make no mistake about it:
We are getting into position
To open the heavy, creaking door of forgiveness.
We are almost there.

This Moment in Time

The trio of open-mouthed O's serenade us,
Singing of how
The generosity of our hearts will be ransomed;
And our deep knowledge of each other will return.

Belleruth Naparstek
Author, teacher, and social worker, Ohio

*   *   *

At this turning point, as at others,

We pause from our struggle to hold on
and relax into the passing of what is no more.

We pause from our sadness
and rest on a carpet of green moss.

We pause from our longing
and drink in the sufficiency of this moment.

We pause from our dread of emptiness
and enter a deeper emptiness: still, luminous and sweet.

At this turning point, as at others,
we take a breath and step forward
unprepared but awake.

And you, dear sister-brother,
from what do you pause
at this turning point, as at others?

John Davis
Teacher, Ridhwan School, Colorado

96

Because the future is here, it never arrives.

We stop, solemn at the lip of a new millennium,
peering into a fog that creeps from horizon to twilight;
wondering what 2000 will bring.

We crouch, anxious 'round the camp fires.
Eyes glazed with the blight
we have spread on, in, under
and beyond the planet.
Fear seeping into the soil of our souls.

We stand, looking for the bright dawn
Longing for the fulsome embrace
Counting on the coming of the kingdom
Calling for the glory of light, love, and
abiding joy to reign.

All the while knowing that
it can only be what we are.
Because the future never arrives.
It is already here.

Puran Perez
The Sufi Way, New Jersey

It is the last day of the "old" millennium.
It is the first day of the "new" millennium.

Do you notice a difference? Is it important?

This day is special because it is *today*.
This moment is special because it is *now,*
    and you are alive, and this moment, like all other mo-
ments,
        is filled to the brim with potential.

In fact, this moment has no brim.

It fills and flows effortlessly into the next moment;
    and into the next, and the next,
        right through the millennial threshold.

        Notice the threshold, of course,
                but don't trip on it.

Soften your eyes to the edges of such imagined boundaries.
Soften your heart as well.
Notice primarily what joins, what is continuous . . .
    from moment to moment, place to place, life form to life
form.
In that continuity dwells the substance of life, the source of
true joy.

Janet Kahn
Sociologist and somatic therapist,
Peace Village Projects, Inc., Maryland

This Moment in Time

Perhaps
for a moment
the typewriters will stop clicking,
the wheels stop rolling,
the computers desist from computing,
and a hush will fall over the city.
For in an instant, in the stillness,
the chiming of celestial spheres will be heard
as earth hangs poised
in the crystalline darkness, and then
gracefully
tilts.

Let there be a season
when holiness is heard, and
the splendor of living is revealed.
Stunned to stillness by beauty
we remember who we are and why we are here.
There are inexplicable mysteries.

We are not alone.
In the universe there moves a Wild One
whose gestures alter earth's axis
toward love.
In the immense darkness
everything spins with joy.

The cosmos enfolds us.
We are caught in a web of stars,
cradled in a swaying embrace,
rocked by the holy night,
babes of the universe.

This Moment in Time

Let this be the time
we wake to life,
as spring wakes,
in the moment of winter solstice.

Rebecca Parker
President, Starr King School for Ministry, California

* * *

"Almost the twenty-first century"—
how quickly the thought will grow dated,
even quaint.

Our hopes, our future,
will pass like the hopes and futures of others.

And all our anxieties and terrors,
nights of sleeplessness,
griefs,
will appear then as they truly are—

Stumbling, delirious bees in the tea scent of jasmine.

Jane Hirshfield
"Jasmine"
Poet, California

Dear World,
18,400 years ago, this comet
we call (in 1996) Hyakutake
came close to the Earth (ten million
miles away, ten million); and we

can see it with the naked
eye, floating in the sky like
a tail of light. The last
time it came within ten million

miles, humans were just crossing
the terrible, icy glaciers,
the Bering Strait, into this
land mass, North America, one

of the floating, enduring Turtles.
The Turtles whispered, "Leap of
faith, dream, leap of faith, dream,"
as the comet edged its way

ten million miles, so close. 18,400
years later, the Turtles whisper,
"Leap of faith, one planet, leap
of faith, one people." This planet

floating through the stars, comets
coming home to sing to the Turtles:
"Cross the terrible, icy glaciers,
the human heart, leap."

Alma Luz Villanueva
Author, California

This Moment in Time

100

*"For in God's sight, a day can mean a thousand years,
and a thousand years is like a day."*
Threshold
No more than a new dawn
Like 100 million other dawns
that have come and gone
*"Each with troubles enough
of its own . . ."*
Yet each day (after day after day)
filled—blessings—miracles—surprises
Still
Threshold
This day as a thousand years
New

Awaken us, O Awakened One
Be Morning Star, O Anointed One
This day is all we have
in which to awaken
To serve and bless
To heal and be—
is enough
*"For any who hear me knocking
let them open, and I will
enter . . ."*

Celeste J. Rossmiller
The Naropa Institute, Colorado

The millennia call out to each other
    across the great divide of time
like a mass of people who arrive at a
      shore and call out to the waves
or to distant fishing boats who
        can't hear them.

102

Each time a century starts
it's an edge.
Enchanted scissors cut time a neat slice
and the start of the year
takes place as if on ice over deep water,
revelers dangerously drunk and disorderly
cut off from the previous people in suddenly
      out-of-fashion clothes and quirks
        and ways of thinking

separated from the forward flow of time
as stiff as mannequins
locked in the show windows
      of the department stores that've gone out of business.

But a giant millennial angel bright as polished pewter
with sweeping yellow wings and face of
    lunar innocence
pulls by and stretches all the way from the
anguished souls of the former century
to the souls, born and unborn, of the next
who somehow think they're
      free of time and responsibility and the
        legacy of the last century

and this delectable angel deftly puts in their eyes
a supernal radiance that shows
that the one heart of humankind
has a single song to sing
to a single Listener

however it may be perceived by the
    six billion crowding the
        planet at the time!

                      Daniel Abdal-Hayy Moore
            Sufi Muslim, poet, Pennsylvania

             ✱   ✱   ✱

New Millennium
Old Millennium,
Time is timeless.
Grasping is futile
Rejecting is painful,
Care lightly and gently.
Like a mother holding a child,
Not too loose, not too tight.

                        Martine Batchelor
     Zen Buddhist teacher, Sharpham College, England

This Moment in Time

Where is this New Millennium? Where on Earth can it be found? What extraordinary creatures we are! We delight or anguish over a dissolving event. What we make of it is what we make of it.

It is not only the notion of a New Millennium that is puzzling, but the corresponding notion that there are countries on this Earth which we think also bear a true reality. Where on Earth are these countries? What a strange species we are, fighting and killing over the notion of countries. Ah, I know what you are thinking. Animals are territorial. They do the same thing. Ah, so are we animals with sophisticated weapons? Do we really wish to protect areas by marking boundaries we have urinated upon?

Where is this New Millennium? Is there anything tangible about it? Is there anything out there in nature that communicates this so-called major event? What strange creatures we are. We wish to impose a non-reality on Earth's simple reality, free from days, decades, years, and countries. Ah, I know what you are thinking. We must celebrate this historical moment. It could help to forge a new beginning. But how could investing in the number 2000 do that?

What is this New Millennium? Nothing more, nothing less than a thought in the mind. With projections, investments, and identification we can make a big event out of a number. Are we going to be like Hollywood stars, clever at being someone that we are not? Clever at projecting ourselves onto a millennium?

Let us be clear; let us be free from the razzmatazz of a number, of a dream world. Let us celebrate instead the ending in our mind of any reality to the vain idea of 2000. Puncture the myth of our New Millennium.

Let us celebrate the ending of numbers and divisions. Let us explode the myth of the nation state and its contribution to urinating upon the Earth.

Let us instead stand together on this wondrous Earth and know our enlightened freedom, untainted by hype and horror.

105

Christopher Titmuss
Dharma teacher, Gaia House, England

*   *   *

The millennium is a painted spot on the ocean
Where once you caught a fish.

Alan Senauke
Buddhist Peace Fellowship, California

May the accolade for the first instant of the new millennium
make us aware of its flip side:
    its precious emptiness.
Let us proclaim, over and over again, that we shall not allow
ourselves to be squeezed in the vise

    of one millennium and the next,
    of past and future,
    of the portentous and the ordinary,
    of success and failure,
    of gain and loss,
    of praise and blame,
    of me and the other.
Freedom is to be discovered outside of such partitions,
and eternity can be found in each grain of time.

José Reissig
Scientist and meditation teacher, New York

Dear god
Is there really anything to it
some significance
some magic
in this 2000?

Sweet deity
Obviously you won't tell us
That's not how it works
There's some glimmer there
something about making our own meaning
no doubt

Here's an invocation then, beloved:
Let us gather
our loves our ties our illusions
our riches our sorrows our poor
our partners children friends
possessions obsessions triumphs mysteries
and carry them like a bride on high
across threshold 2000

And let us marvel
that in this world
where nobody agrees on anything
and everything is too precious to be left undisputed
millions of us
still agree that it is the year 2000

Kiran Rana
Publisher, Hunter House, California

This Moment in Time

Millennium schmillennium—
the time is Now
Are you waiting for The Revolution?
kickin' back too busy tired
like, consciousness is really gonna track you down
beneath 9 to 5 and compromise
knocking on your door with 2 tickets to
The New Jerusalem.
On your feet!
Stretch
walk 'n' pray
carry
Your Love
to
the streets
and smile!
Millenniums happen in a
stride
a choice
a gesture
Now.

Danielle LaPorte
Co-director, The Next Level, Washington, D.C.

. . . We light a narrow candle
for every turn around our little sun. make a wish
and try to blow them out in a single breath.
between the near stars and the ones we take on faith
there is no middle distance. no halfway measure
of the years they say light takes to get here.
souls are said to journey from other lives to get to
this one through what we call living here then
on to the next thing we don't have names for.
there appears to be no reason to hurry.
no need to fear we're going too fast.
we travel in constant nearness. it is always now.
we are here, then we are here.
the farther we go the more we are home . . .

109

Jerry Martien
"Cake and Ice Cream"
Poet, California

At night I wait for a sign
in the wind, a stillness
in the cold, black water
before jumping
from the rocky ledge,
knowing my body must
find its way through darkness.
I begin each dive like the first time—
a whispered invocation.

Amy Uyematsu
Teacher and poet, California

*   *   *

We have eaten of the world.
Molecules of chaos and chance
reign in our bodies.
You are cast in the river
to dwell in the transformation.

Holly St. John Bergon
Poet and professor, New York

110

Why this earth
in solemn patterns
turns
why this sun
circles nightly
casting shadows across the sinking front porch
swing
why this woman
in holy wonder
repeats the human story
why this child
grows in beauty
laughs and cries
lives
turning never escaping
this simple narrative spins us
into reflections
versions of each other

turning turning
we watch
as brightly shines the moon

111

Kateri Damm
Poet, Canada

112

On the first evening
buzzing with the last light
that skids through everything,
let the body drink its deepest
breath, the lower back
spreading like a constellation
with one lone star swerving.
Let the hands, lined with meteors,
open, releasing all they have held—
coins, hammers, steering
wheels, and the silken
faces of children—to find
what on earth they really hold.
Let the crown of the head
move away from the shoulders
and into the distance
where another is waiting.
Let go of the forecast you heard
when you were younger
than the child now clattering
up the backstairs all
laughter and gasping
for what we're here to do.
Look down. Look at the stars.
We're here so briefly, weather
with bones.

Wyatt Townley
"Prayer for a New Millennium"
Poet, Kansas

Let's dress up in feathered gowns, saffron robes, bison skins
　　　and welcome another chilead dawning
Let's put on the thunder god mask, praise the loon, the
　　　rhapsodist's calling

Let's celebrate our caudate line—bacteria, fishes, bamboo-
　　munchers,
　　　musicians, monks, military men, merchants, mailmen,
　　　　all the monkey-footed
　　　　　　—let's bring them in to share our grain

113

Let's prowl fir hangers in lynx-tufted ears—
　　　wolves will return if we make them welcome, grizzlies
　　　　　too,
　　　snowshoe hares & caribou—
　　　　　let's open the woods to the wolverine

Let's wake up! Sun in our eyes—
　　　without a text, without a prayer—
　　　we've scaled, we've flaked, we've sharpened tools
　　　we've cried war chants for ten-thousand years,
　　　now it's time to shut up & listen:
　　　caught between drought and fatal rain,
　　　it's time to sit, to watch the breath,
　　　now it's time to keep ourselves still—

　　　　Red-lidded eyes, hogback ridge,
　　　　　At day's first glow, paws in the mud—

Let dawn's white dogs howl up the sun.

Fred Ferraris
Poet and builder, Colorado

Enough. These few words are enough.
If not these words, this breath.
If not this breath, this sitting here.

This opening to the life
we have refused
again and again
until now.

Until now.

David Whyte
Poet, Washington State

*   *   *

A child stood on his seat in a restaurant,
holding the railing of the chairback
as though to address a courtroom,

"Nobody knows what's going to happen next."

Then his turning-slide back down to his food,
relieved and proud to say the truth,
as were we to hear it.

Coleman Barks
"The Railing"
Poet and translator, Georgia

Part 4

CREATING
COMMUNITIES
of PEACE

There lies before us, if we choose, continued
progress in happiness, knowledge, and wis-
dom. Shall we, instead, choose death, because
we cannot forget our quarrels? We appeal, as
human beings, to human beings: Remember
your humanity and forget the rest.

ALBERT EINSTEIN

While history is inscribed with the names of famous leaders, it is not primarily through the actions of individuals that we have survived to this time, but rather through the actions of communities. We are social animals, and only through co-operation and communication have we been able to survive the wars, famines, pogroms, plagues, and natural disasters that beset us. Community is our basic strategy of survival and evolution.

Community means the strength of unity to do the work that needs to be done. It means arms to hold us when we falter, a circle of healing, a circle of friends, someplace where we can most be ourselves. Of course, communities are not always so supportive. Some communities, in order to maintain their cohesiveness, enact strict rules of identity and behavior, fortifying themselves against the "other"—whoever is different from themselves. This suspicion goes by many names: sectarianism, localism, tribalism, classism, nationalism, xenophobia, racism. Whatever the label, self-protective suspicion serves to unify a subgroup at the expense of the larger community.

It is a natural desire to join with those who think or look like us. Perhaps we feel more at ease with "our own kind." But the health and strength of our communities and nations depend on our tolerance of diversity, not our sameness. The prayers in Part 4 urge us to open ourselves to the possibility of true coexistence with people who seem different, people we do not understand and whose views we do not share. How can we do this? How can we overcome suspicion and distrust?

We asked this question of the great Cambodian monk Maha Ghosananda, a man who has done more than any other to heal the spirit of his divided country. His response was threefold: first, release your judgments and recognize that you do not know this "other"; second, ask questions—ask what matters to those who are different from you, ask about their suffering; and third, listen with respect and an open heart. If you do these things, the process of reconciliation and peace is begun.

Each of us knows that opening to the truth and presence of the "other" is not always easy.

> The hardest part is people.
> Lord, help me face them
> without rancor or disappointment.
> Help me see the pain behind their actions
> rather than the malice;
> the suffering rather than the rage.

Karen Holden

This practice requires us to be rooted in our common humanity rather than isolated in our separate identity or group. It asks us to recognize that one of the main things we share is our diversity, and that these differences—though real—need not threaten our own identity or truth. Coexistence requires us to see the interdependent nature of all communities and to learn respect for all voices, allowing (even encouraging) them to be heard. Yes, the message of some voices may feel dangerous to the larger community, but if we listen with respect and compassion, we can change the nature of our encounter from opposition to reconciliation. In accepting life's natural diversity, we can find what we hold in common and build bridges that enable our mutual work to continue.

You, the one
From whom on different paths
All of us have come,

To whom on different paths
All of us are going,
Make strong in our hearts what unites us;

Build bridges across all that divides us;
United make us rejoice in our diversity,

At one in our witness to your peace,
A rainbow of your glory.
Amen.

Br. David Steindl-Rast, O.S.B.
Mount Saviour Monastery, New York

120

We will plant olive trees
where before
there were thorns.

All of us the same,
each one of us different,
we will walk hand in hand
with a new song
of love on our lips.

We will plant olive trees
where before
there were thorns.

Sharing
is the one urgent need
in this dawning
of a new century.

Paz, peace, paix,
mir, shalom, salaam:
we will plant olive trees
where before
there were thorns!

Federico Mayor
Spanish Director General, UNESCO, France

Ah——
I be your shelter
I be your land
I be your everything
I be your friend
I be your water——
when you're thirsty and dry

122

The way before me was mine to make
There was no road no path to take
As I hacked my life through this muddy rocked way
Others toiled beside me for a justice new day
Still I have felt lonely most of the time
Walking this sweet freedom struggle of mine

Yesterday I stumbled around a bend
I saw you standing, you reached me your hand
I'd seen you before, oh many a time
Why, your life had plowed the row right next to mine
But now you make the sun rise in my sky
You rock my cradle honey, you made me fly
You keep me company

Ah——
I be your shelter
I be your land
I be your everything
I be your friend
I be your water——
when you're thirsty and dry

Bernice Johnson Reagon
Singer, composer, and historian, Washington, D.C.

The Arabs used to say,
When a stranger appears at your door,
feed him for three days
before asking who he is,
where he's come from,
where he's headed.
That way, he'll have strength enough
to answer.
Or, by then you'll be such good friends
you don't care.

Let's go back to that.
Rice? Pine nuts?
Here, take the red brocade pillow.
My child will serve water
to your horse.

No, I was not busy when you came!
I was not preparing to be busy.
That's the armor everyone put on
at the end of the century
to pretend they had a purpose
in the world.

I refuse to be claimed.
Your plate is waiting.
We will snip fresh mint
into your tea.

Naomi Shihab Nye
Author, Texas

Creating Communities of Peace

They are all children when they sleep.
There is no war in them.
They open their hands and breathe
in the slow rhythm given to humans by heaven.

Whether soldiers, statesmen, servants, or masters
they purse their lips like small children
and they all half-open their hands.
Stars stand watch then and the arch of the sky is hazed over
for a few hours when no one will harm another.

If only we could talk with each other then,
when hearts are like half-open flowers.
Words would push their way in
like golden bees.

—God, teach me sleep's language.

124

Rolf Jacobsen
Poet, Norway
Translated by Glenn Storhaug

Together, one with one, we can build the new Earth, a place of wholeness in diversity. We can transform our organizations into communities, places of compassion and care.

Our leaders will focus on affirming and renewing values, building community, and releasing human possibilities. Connection, not acquisition, will be seen as the primary human motivator. The core question will be, How can I help?

Together, we will build spaces of renewal, creating safe places in dysfunctional organizations, seedbeds for a new world. We will advocate a new leadership based on service above self. We will replace the leader on top of our pyramid with a leadership circle, moving beyond the rhetoric of participation to shared governance in fact.

In calling forth this new day, let us be guided by our hearts to be the vessels for the light that powers the Universe, to be a chord in the one song of our healed and holy Home.

John Jacob Gardiner
Professor of Leadership, Seattle University, Washington

We all drink from one water
We all breathe from one air
We rise from one ocean
And we live under one sky

Remember
We are one

The newborn baby cries the same
The laughter of children is universal
Everyone's blood is red
And our hearts beat the same song

Remember
We are one

We are all brothers and sisters
Only one family, only one earth
Together we live
And together we die

Remember
We are one

Peace be on you
Brothers and Sisters
Peace be on you

Anwar Fazal
Recipient, Right Livelihood Award, Malaysia

May we remember, as we log on, that half the world's people have never used a telephone, and recall, as we chatter, that most of those around us have no chance to speak or move as they choose. May we recall that more than a billion beings live without food, and that as many children live amidst poverty and war.

May we have the strength to question our own gods, and the grace to respect others'; may we, on a globe that is shrinking and expanding, honor our differences, while finding a language in which to speak of them together. May we recall that the responsibility of the fortunate is to answer the prayers of others, and the privilege of the blessed is to make cause for general gratitude; may we sing hymns for the opportunities we often ignore and say hallelujahs to the moments that are everyday gifts.

May we speak to the best in our neighbors and attend to the worst in ourselves; may we have the courage to leaven compassion with discernment, and the sense to make knowledge dance with innocence.

May we, above all, in the clamor of the moment, find a space to recollect what we treasure, and a silence in which to recall the fact that progress, fundamentally, takes us backward, toward the essential and the deep. And may we continue, amidst the acceleration and opportunities of the moment, to see what exists beyond all moments, and to rejoice in the wise souls in our midst (and in these pages) whose challenges and injunctions and reminders answer our petitions and our needs, while leaving us with questions it is our duty—our pleasure— to take home.

Pico Iyer
Author, California

Almighty and Eternal God, the father in the Parable of the Prodigal Son clearly manifests your dispositions toward us. Thus you forgave the Prodigal Son for his frantic pursuit of pleasure, for squandering the rich inheritance you had given him. You forgave the Elder Son for his self-righteous condemnation both of his younger brother and of your tender forgiveness of his outrageous behavior. You insisted only that they live together in peace. May we know your infinite mercy and share it with one another both as individuals and as nations, races, religions, ethnic groups, neighbors, households, and families. Grant us an ever-deepening commitment to the rights and needs of every member of the human family and an ever-increasing respect and love for the integrity and interdependence of all creation.

Abbot Thomas Keating, O.C.S.O.
Saint Benedict's Monastery, Colorado

O God, help us in this darkened period of human history to remember once again who we are and what the purpose of our existence is here on earth. We have become usurpers of the human state, parading as human beings without full awareness of what it really means to be human. Rather than being a channel of Thy grace for Thy creation, we have decimated the harmony of life on earth, pushing many of the species (including ours) to the verge of extinction.

O God, awaken us at the beginning of this new era from the dream of negligence and help us to fulfill our responsibilities as representatives of Thy sovereignty here on earth with essential duties toward each other and toward the whole of creation. Help us to remember our true nature, to recall whence we came and whither we shall go. Aid us in the journey of life to do Thy will and to act as the bridge between Heaven and earth, thus fulfilling the role for which Thou didst create us. Shower Thy grace upon us in the moment of our greatest need, protect us from ourselves, and allow us to be a beacon of light rather than a dark cloud for the ambience that surrounds us. Only with Thy aid can we create that peace within and harmony with the outer environment, both natural and social, for which our souls yearn. Only awareness of Thy oneness can prevent us from that idolatry and dispersive multiplicity that destroy all that our inner being seeks. We pray to Thee to help us remain true to our inner selves, to that primordial nature which we still carry in the deep recesses of our souls.

Seyyed Hossein Nasr
Professor of Islamic Studies,
George Washington University, Washington, D.C.

In this century and in any century,
Our deepest hope, our most tender prayer,
Is that we learn to listen.
May we listen to one another in openness and mercy
May we listen to plants and animals in wonder and respect
May we listen to our own hearts in love and forgiveness
May we listen to God in quietness and awe.
And in this listening,
Which is boundless in its beauty,
May we find the wisdom to cooperate
With a healing spirit, a divine spirit,
Who beckons us into peace and community and creativity.
We do not ask for a perfect world.
But we do ask for a better world.
We ask for deep listening.

Jay McDaniel
Professor of Religion, Hendrix College, Arkansas

130

We are women and men of the millennium
We are wisdom and creativity embodied,
a voice for Gaia's energy unfolding.
We are community—
discerning, empowering, and compassionate,
interconnected with all beings.
We are change,
encouraging inner and outer healing,
willing to be in the cauldron of transformation.
We are willing to recognize our wholeness and holiness,
willing to grow with peace, power, and love.
We are witness to the pain and injustice around us,
willing to be companions in the struggle.
We believe in equality and diversity,
respecting differences.
We believe that giving is the act of receiving,
that in healing ourselves
we heal our world.
We believe that we are interconnected,
part of ancestors and children to come,
part of soil, earth, and stars.

Pat Cane
Human rights activist, Capacitar, California

We praise You, God of all the earth,
and all Your ways we bless.
In You all love begins and ends.
Your universal love transcends
our own dividedness.

We call to You with words we clothe
in cultures of our own.
You rise above all cultic claims
to answer to our many names,
a God as yet unknown.

O Wisdom, wait within us,
wake our weary hearts to praise,
empowering the powerless
and strengthening with gentleness,
'till all embrace Your ways.

Our many paths all lead to You
in every time and place.
Our hearts rejoice in serving You.
Make all we are and all we do
a channel of Your grace.

We turn to You, O Sacred Source
of hope and harmony.
Our work on earth will not be done,
'till human hearts all beat as one
in global unity.

Miriam Therese Winter
Medical Mission Sisters, Connecticut

The spiritual world is like the natural world—only diversity will save it. Just as the health of a forest or fragrant meadow can be measured by the number of different insects and plants and creatures that successfully make it their home, so only by an extraordinary abundance of disparate spiritual and philosophic paths will human beings navigate a pathway through the dark and swirling storms that mark our current era. "Not by one avenue alone," wrote Symmachus sixteen centuries ago, "can we arrive at so tremendous a secret."

Margot Adler
Journalist and commentator, New York

*   *   *

The main task of the immediate future is to assist in activating the inter-communication of all the living and non-living components of the earth community in what can be considered the emerging ecological period of earth development. Functionally the great art of achieving this historical goal is the art of intimacy and distance, the capacity of beings to be totally present to each other while further affirming and enhancing the differences and identities of each.

Thomas Berry
Cultural historian, North Carolina

Come, friends. Let us gather.
Let us assemble, and speak.
We have here the Talking Circle.
Great are its mysteries.
Come, then, let us be seated.
Let us see what comes of it.
Do you hear the silence?
The silence is the secret.
The secret is sacred.
Because of the Circle we have words.
With our words we break the silence.
Breaking the silence releases
The secrets.
This is how the mysteries
Are revealed.
Mysteries are forever.
Come, then. Let us gather.
Let us assemble, and speak.

Richard Doiron
Poet, Canada

Father/Mother God, Holy Spirit

Help us to stay connected to our hearts and each other.
Help us to see the good in ourselves and each other.
Help us to serve the spirit of goodness in all we meet.
Help us, especially, to recognize our connection to those
    who think themselves our enemy.
Help us to find value in our connection to those
    whom we might think our enemies.
Help us to restore love upon this earth.
May all be fed.
May all be healed.
May all be loved.

John Robbins
Author, EarthSave International, Kentucky

May we recognize the Spirit
in each of us, and the Spirit
in all of us.

Ram Dass
Teacher and author, Hanuman Foundation, California

136

I pray for a world where all people learn to think of "I and Thou," practice "existence and coexistence" and move through life individually and with others, woven together, separate yet interconnected, like the light and dark of the Tao.

I pray for a world where all children are taught about coexistence, cooperation, and community-building at an early age; that they learn tolerance and respect and can overcome the prejudice they learn from adults.

I pray for a world where difference, tradition, culture, and spiritual roots are honored, where the goal of peaceful coexistence is as important as clean air, clean water, and protecting all the species on earth.

I pray for a world where political leaders encourage respect for diversity instead of exploiting differences for political gain.

I pray for a world where leaders of all faiths denounce absolutism and fundamentalism, where respect and tolerance for all expressions of connectivity with God or the Universal Spirit are understood as expressions of our shared desire to join with a Higher Power.

I pray for a planet where the oppression of minorities is universally condemned, where we can all coexist rather than become extinct; a world where the ideals of coexistence and community-building become educational priorities and shared societal goals.

Alan Slifka
Chairman and co-founder, The Abraham Fund, New York

If nations are to live, they must have among them a group of people who raise the challenge of right and wrong. In every century we find people who dedicate their lives to guiding others. Where no such group is found, the people perish and chaos and corruption spread.

Those who put right what is wrong save nations from destruction. They are doctors of humanity. A sick person who does not find a doctor, or does not take the doctor's advice, will die. This is the relationship between nations and those who set out to change them.

Nobility of person, springing from high morals—this character trait is the only factor strong enough to spread the spirit of peace and tolerance. People blessed with this trait bring a new orientation to end tyranny, remove bitterness from the human heart, and stop the mad rush toward materialism.

Let us pray that we shall see the day when ordinary people, responsible leaders, and indeed all world statesmen work together to put an end to selfishness. Then by God's grace our world will be set free from its present bitterness and fear.

Shaikh Mohammed Ahmad Surur
Eritrea

It is no longer news that we live in an era of radical change, where few people retain a pure genetic strain or remain through a lifetime in the same locale. Our world today is nearly unrecognizable tomorrow, and generations last at most ten years. All we know or ever knew has been transformed. Every thought, every land, every connection is not what it used to be. We live on a globe where a person's symbolic world—once largely circumscribed by region or nation, one's own tribe, religion, class, or race—today is defined by the globe as a whole.

Today, in recognizing the intimate connectedness of all creation—in the revelations of contemporary physics and the global immediacy of the Internet—we the human species simply must acknowledge and embrace the many rich sacred traditions our sisters and brothers have uplifted in awe and wonder throughout the ages.

My prayer, my hope, my faith for all creatures who dwell upon this earth in the centuries to come is grounded on the bedrock belief that *only* if we humans draw upon the strengths of the world's many religions and spiritual traditions will our children, our species, and the planet herself survive. It is not an original thought. Many of our greatest minds, including those in this volume, recognize the primal place of the universal experience that binds us (as in the root of the word *religion: religare,* to bind). It is this binding, the recognition of the oneness in all its diversity of expression, that is the basis of "interfaith."

I am often asked, What is interfaith? Most fundamentally, interfaith is *respect*. Respect for different traditions, different religions, different faiths. It is coming to understand them. And more, it is coming to love them. All of us have so many layers in our lives. We speak many languages and listen to diverse music. We eat many different kinds of food. It is time that our spiritual diet, too, becomes a healthy mixed menu. Its very variety makes us richer, deeper, more understanding, more loving.

It is time to come together in respect, understanding, and the common breaking of our many daily breads together. Our shared words of faith must be these: *communion* (not conversion), *respect, and love with compassion.*

Very Rev. James Parks Morton
President, Interfaith Center of New York

Hidden, eternal, unfathomable, all-merciful God,
beside you there is no other God.
You are great and worthy of all praise;
your power and grace sustain the universe.

God of faithfulness without falsity, just and truthful,
you chose Abraham, your devout servant,
to be the father of many nations,
and you have spoken through the prophets.
Hallowed and praised be your name throughout the world.
May your will be done wherever people live.

Living and gracious God, hear our prayer;
our guilt has become great.
Forgive us children of Abraham our wars,
our enmities, our misdeeds toward one another.
Rescue us from all distress and give us peace.

Guardian of our destiny,
bless the leaders and rulers of the nations,
that they may not covet power and glory
but act responsibly
for the welfare and peace of humankind.
Guide our religious communities and those set over them,
that they may not only proclaim the message of peace
but also show it in their lives.
And to all of us, and to those who do not worship among us,
give your grace, mercy, and all good things,
and lead us, God of the living,
on the right way to your eternal glory.

Hans Küng, "An Invocation for Jews, Christians, and Muslims"
President, Foundation for Global Ethics, Switzerland

Creating Communities of Peace

Friendship toward all beings,
Delight in the qualities of virtuous ones,
Utmost compassion for afflicted beings,
Equanimity toward those who are not
    well-disposed toward me.

May my soul have such dispositions as these forever.

Peacefulness toward all beings;
self-control and pure aspirations;
abandonment of every thought
that is tainted by desire or aversion;
that, truly, is dwelling in my Self.

I ask forgiveness of all living creatures,
May all of them forgive me.
May I have a friendly relationship with all beings
and unfriendly with none.

Padmanabh S. Jaini
"A Jain Prayer"
Professor, University of California at Berkeley

Loaf-baking, kitchen-dwelling, breast-feeding God,
hungry and thirsty
we return to your lap and your table again.
Fill us with bread that satisfies,
milk that drenches our parched throats.
Feed us 'til we want no more.

142

Let your Spirit hang an apron around our necks.
Fashioned by our Lord and friend, Jesus.

Instruct us,
here in the halls of your kitchen-kingdom,
with the recipes: mercy and forgiveness,
compassion and redemption.
Leaven our lives
'til they rise in praise:
Offered, blessed, and broken
for the healing of the nations.

Rev. Ken Sehested
Baptist Peace Fellowship of North America, North Carolina

You—
The power of creation
Giver of life—
Guide us on our way.
Where there is pain—
Bring comfort. You!
Where there is hunger—
Bring food. You!
Where there is quarrel—
Bring love. You!
You—
All of us together!

Bruno Manser
Defender of the Penan people, Switzerland

O Wakan Tanka, Creator of the Universe, Maker of All Good Things, Most Compassionate One, Ever-Forgiving One, Most Tender One, Source of All Life, we invoke Your Holy and Everlasting Spirit with our hearts overflowing with praise and thanksgiving through the transforming power of your Sacred Grace and Love.

And through the Power of this Sacred Grace and Love we summon, from that direction from which comes the warmth of the dawning Red Sunrise, all the tribes and nations of the East, to join their hearts and minds together in everlasting love, peace, unity, kindness, and understanding.

And from that direction from which comes New Life and where the Yellow Sun stands in its greatest strength, we summon all the tribes and nations of the South to join their hearts and minds together in everlasting love, peace, unity, kindness, and understanding.

And from that direction from which come Thunder, Lightning, Rain, and Darkness, we summon all the tribes and Nations of the West to join their hearts and minds together in everlasting love, peace, unity, kindness, and understanding.

And from that direction from which come the White Snow and the Purifying North Winds, we summon all the tribes and nations of the north to join their hearts and minds together in everlasting love, peace, unity, kindness, and understanding.

And to Father Sky, where the white swans, hawks, geese, and eagles fly and from where the Sun, the Moon, and the Stars illumine all created things, we offer Thanksgiving and humbly implore that we may experience what it means to be a good grandson, a good son, a good father, a good grandfather, a good friend, and a good husband.

And to Mother Earth, where the mineral, plant, animal, and human people live and from where the Sacred Rivers flow, we offer Thanksgiving and humbly implore that we may experience what it means to be a good granddaughter, a good daughter, a good mother, a good grandmother, a good friend and a good wife.

And from the very center of our hearts and our innermost beings, we offer Thanksgiving for all of life's perfecting experiences, past, present, and future, with complete faith that all the Sacred Teachings, Prophecies, and Potentialities of the Four Directions will be fully realized, while always remembering that the Center of the Universe is Everywhere.

Philip Lane, Jr.
"Prayers for the Sacred Directions"
Yankton Dakota and Chickasaw nations, North America

O Ajau, Tepeu, Qu Kumatz, Heart of Heaven, Heart of Earth, Heart of Air, Heart of Water, Ajau, Hun Ajpu, two, three times father, two, three times grandfather, Sun of Suns, Light of Lights, Giver of sons and daughters, Giver of wealth, we praise You, we glorify You wherever we are, on roads, in canyons, by the banks of rivers, at the ocean's edge, underneath trees, by rocks, on volcanoes, on mountaintops; we pray to You for our life, for our children's lives, for those of our future generations. Grant us our successors while there is yet light, while there is yet clarity, while the sun shines. The canopy of heaven, sacred bundle of humanity, have pity on us. May You turn Your glory and majesty toward us. May our elders the trees return, may our brothers and sisters the animals return, may pure air flow, that there may be life. Strengthen my wise elders, and may my valiant warriors be strong, those who defend the colors of Your beauty, so that it may never fade.

Your name shall be on their lips, O Ajau.

* * *

Awaken, America! Look at your sky; look at your stars; look at your clouds; look at your Earth, your lakes, your rivers, your volcanoes, your valleys. Shall it be only our life that we value, or shall we consider that of our children? Are we the only children of this planet, or are there others? The Mayan prophecy is being fulfilled. Arise; may all arise. No one shall be left behind. May dawn come; may the new day begin, so that the people may have peace and be happy.

Awaken, America! The Mayan prophecy says, awaken! It is now time for the dawn, and the work shall be completed. The time, measured by time, when what has been written in the pyramids shall be fulfilled, has come. The time of 12 Baktun,

13 Ajau. You in your language, and me in mine; you with your belief, and me with my culture. We are all called, rich and poor, black and white, indigenous and nonindigenous. We have one single sun that illuminates us, one single air that nourishes us, one single water that we drink and that becomes the blood that flows in our veins, and one single Mother Earth where we live, whom we must defend.

don Alejandro Cirilo Perez Oxlaj
Mayan priest, Guatemala

*   *   *

May goddess flow again through
the dried-up riverbeds of human minds.
May she well up once more from the
blocked springs of human hearts.
May she dance with courage in
office blocks and railway stations and
through virtual space around the world,
dissolving hierarchies and creating
at last a genuine deep equality for
all members of the human race.

Jocelyn Chaplin
Teacher, artist, and psychotherapist, England

We call upon our Ancestors,
Spirit of the earth we walk upon,
Spirit of the universe.

We have come to a crossroad,
to a time when every word matters,
to a time when we must reevaluate ourselves and our actions.

Our heart is fragile
our body is shivering in front of the unknown
our back is heavy with past burdens
burdens we do not know how to be rid of.

We ask that you shower us once again with love and
    compassion
make peace rain on our heart and soul
teach us how to see each other with a brand-new eye
help us to appreciate and welcome each other.

We need your blessings to move on,
we need your strength to make it through this time of
    turbulence.
Ancestors, hold us in your peace and warmth.

Sobonfu and Malidoma Somé
Teachers and ritual guides, Burkina Faso, Africa

Creating Communities of Peace

The hardest part is people.
So Lord, help me face them
without rancor or disappointment.
Help me see the pain behind their actions
rather than the malice;
the suffering rather than the rage.

And in myself, as I struggle
with the vise of my own desire—
give me strength to quiet my heart,
to quicken my empathy, to act
in gratitude rather than need.

Remind me that the peace I find
in the slow track of seasons
or an uncurling fern frond,
is married to the despair I feel
in the face of nuclear war.

Remind me that each small bird shares atoms
with anthrax, with tetanus, with acid rain,
that each time I close my heart
to another, I add to the darkness;
Help me always follow kindness.

Let this be my prayer.

149

Karen Holden
Poet and teacher,
Frank Lloyd Wright School
of Architecture, Arizona

The stunning paradox of human spiritual maturity is that, as we become one with all creation, we also at the same time become completely and uniquely ourselves.

Thomas Yeomans
Psychologist, Massachusetts

*   *   *

Han-shan, that great and crazy, wonder-filled
Chinese poet of a thousand years ago, said:

We're just like bugs in a bowl. All day
going around never leaving their bowl.

I say: That's right! Every day climbing up
the steep sides, sliding back.

Over and over again. Around and around.
Up and back down.

Sit in the bottom of the bowl, head in your hands,
cry, moan, feel sorry for yourself.

Or. Look around. See your fellow bugs.
Walk around.

Say, Hey, how you doin'?
Say, Nice bowl!

David Budbill
"Bugs in a Bowl"
Poet, Vermont

Creating Communities of Peace

What are we doing here in this meadow?
We are measuring ourselves among the vanishing grasses.
What am I doing, now, on this shore?
I am counting myself among the broken shells.
What are we doing here in this forest?
We are remembering our families beside the trees.
What am I doing at dawn on these waters?
I am recalling my cousins beyond the waves.

What are we doing here in this desert?
We are tracing lost paths along the dunes.
What am I doing in morning light on this ice?
I am singing to the future across high winds.
What are we doing here in this field?
With our children, we are gleaning.
What am I doing at noon on this mountain?
With my children, I am tending our few animals.
What are we doing here in this village?
We are gathering.
What am I doing in afternoon sun on this marsh?
I am holding still.
What are we doing here in this town?
We are moving through shattered walls.
What am I doing at dusk on this farm?
I am drawing water from a dwindling well.
What are we doing here in this busy city?
We are listening to angry voices in the dark air.
And what am I doing at eventide on this Earth?
I am taking your hand, making a change.

Hillel Schwartz
Senior Fellow, The Millennium Institute (VA), California

The people I love the best
jump into work head first
without dallying in the shallows
and swim off with sure strokes almost out of sight.
They seem to become natives of that element,
the black sleek heads of seals
bouncing like half-submerged balls.

I love people who harness themselves, an ox to a heavy cart,
who pull like water buffalo, with massive patience,
who strain in the mud and the muck to move things forward,
who do what has to be done, again and again.

I want to be with people who submerge
in the task, who go into the fields to harvest
and work in a row and pass the bags along,
who stand in the line and haul in their places,
who are not parlor generals and field deserters
but move in a common rhythm
when the food must come in or the fire be put out.

The work of the world is common as mud.
Botched, it smears the hands, crumbles to dust.
But the thing worth doing well done
has a shape that satisfies, clean and evident.
Greek amphoras for wine or oil,
Hopi vases that held corn, are put in museums,
but you know they were made to be used.
The pitcher cries for water to carry
and a person for work that is real.

Marge Piercy
Poet and author, Vermont

Creating Communities of Peace

Part 5

FOR *the*
CHILDREN

What are our prayers for the future if not prayers for the children? Our care for our children and for the promise of their lives is as natural to us as breathing. This bond and commitment is in our blood and bones; it is hidden in the seeds deep within our bodies. It is the covenant of our species: to protect and nurture our young, and to prepare a good way for them. We of the living generations are here only because our ancestors remained loyal to this covenant.

So it is agonizing for us to acknowledge the failures we see in modern society's broken covenant with future generations.

> Never have we pushed so many children on to the tumultuous sea of life without the life vests of nurturing families and communities, caring schools, challenged minds, job prospects, and hope.
>
> *Marian Wright Edelman*

We may claim that this is an exaggeration, that it is someone else's problem, not ours. But if we look deeply, we must be chastened by the diminishing prospects and outright threats to the well-being of future generations on every continent. The cohesiveness of family and community bonds is being lost in country after country due to economic stresses; the character provided by diverse cultural heritages is being eclipsed by a global, commercial monoculture; educational systems are underfunded or irrelevant; increasing intolerance and racism confront minority children; health care is all too often lacking

156

or inadequate; the personal and ethical guidance that once was the duty of parents and community has been over-whelmed by television and commercial messages in which one's worth is measured by brand-name products. The litany continues, including the grim, collective inheritance of radioactive waste, nuclear and biological weapons, the spread of overcrowded and poorly designed cities, the loss of wild lands and wildlife, the depletion of soils, and so on and on—an inheritance too depressing to admit yet too insistent to ignore.

It may seem strange to read the preceding paragraph in a book dedicated to expressions of hope for the future. But if nothing else, our children demand honesty from us. We must practice not going into denial, learning instead to sustain our gaze at the dangers around us so that we can respond authentically and creatively. We must let our love for the children keep us from cynicism, despair, and sentimentality—for they will not be fooled. They will come to know either that we told them (and ourselves) the truth and worked for their benefit, or that we avoided the truth and betrayed them. The choice is ours.

The human family has immense reserves of love and ingenuity—more than enough to heal the wounds inflicted on the earth and ourselves. As we nurture our own children, as we help to create supportive communities, as we seek to make our work beneficial to all beings, we participate in the necessary healing.

There is a guide for us in the tasks ahead. Our faithfulness to our children, who are all children everywhere, shows us the way. Offering our prayers for them, and listening to their prayers, we remember the beauty and dependable satisfactions that make life worth living and that keep hope alive.

The infant's delicate forehead a beacon of promise,
his perfect human face, all that we are
depends on him, his stare from another world,
his great, unblinking eyes so new to earth.

The miraculous one keeps rising among us.
Now do we turn and rush to prepare the way.

Anthony Piccione

157

For the Children

You live inside us, beings of the future.

In the spiral ribbons of our cells, you are here. In our rage for the burning forests, the poisoned fields, the oil-drowned seals, you are here. You beat in our hearts through late-night meetings. You accompany us to clear-cuts and toxic dumps and the halls of the lawmakers. It is you who drive our dogged labors to save what is left.

O you who will walk this Earth when we are gone, stir us awake. Behold through our eyes the beauty of this world. Let us feel your breath in our lungs, your cry in our throat. Let us see you in the poor, the homeless, the sick. Haunt us with your hunger, hound us with your claims, that we may honor the life that links us.

You have as yet no faces we can see, no names we can say. But we need only hold you in our mind, and you teach us patience. You attune us to measures of time where healing can happen, where soil and souls can mend. You reveal courage within us we had not suspected, love we had not owned.

O you who come after, help us remember: we are your ancestors. Fill us with gladness for the work that must be done.

Joanna Macy
Buddhist activist and teacher, California

For the Children

I want to be a dogfish
and catch a leaping catfish
with whiskers as long as a stream.
And I want to be
the rain trinkling down on the world
telling it it's springtime.

Noah Frank
Grade 2, Lakeshore Elementary School, California

*   *   *

Children will see it first—
Their sharp eyes and keen hearts
Fixed on a peaceful future.

Youngsters will recognize it unaided—
The earth flowing with milk and honey
Governments cooperating to make sure all are fed.

The little ones of every land—
Gather to grow into the vision.
We who chart the future can only dream.

Let it begin now and let it last long—

Mary E. Hunt
Co-director, Women's Alliance for Theology,
Ethics, and Ritual (WATER), Maryland

For the Children

Imagine living on the coast of West Africa.
In the warm and cheerful climate of Ghana.
Your hair is short and kinky.
Your eyes are big and beautiful.
Your skin is black and shiny
    like the moonless sky on a clear night.
Every day you pray for peace on this earth.

160

Imagine living in the high mountains of North Vietnam.
Surrounded by rice, corn, cassava, and fruit trees.
Your hair is dark and covered with a scarf.
Your eyes are alert and happy.
Your skin is yellow and sparkling
    like the very sun that gives us life.
Every day you pray for peace on this earth.

Imagine living in the Amazon rainforest.
In the humid, temperate Brazilian woods.
Your hair is lush and wavy.
Your eyes are curious and grinning.
Your skin is brown and radiant
    like the soil that nourishes your crops.
Every day you pray for peace on this earth.

Imagine living in the Arctic Circle.
Enjoying the polar nights of Finland.
Your hair is red and silky smooth.
Your eyes are joyous and light.
Your skin is freckled and white
    like a bed of new-fallen snow.
Every day you pray for peace on this earth.

For the Children

Imagine living in the Navajo Nation.
On the plateaus and in the canyons of the dry Arizona desert.
Your hair is long and dark.
Your eyes are alive and dancing.
Your skin is red and weathered
    like the earth of the very land we live on.
Every day you pray for peace on this earth.

161

Kristi Venditti
Student, University of Colorado

O̲ur children, their children, all children
    will intermingle their laughter
      throughout the world
    they'll be as the rainbow
color and hope for the coming dawn.
Kia tou te Rang i marie.

Pauline E. Tangiora
Kaitiaki, Rongomaiwahine Tribe
Aotearoa/New Zealand

For the Children

Spirit of human wisdom, hear my dream! I dream for the next millennium that the care and nurture of our most precious earth's children will take precedence over all else. Help us acknowledge that dreaming and hoping alone will not make it happen. Laws must be changed. Our understanding of a child as a possession must be changed. Thought patterns must be changed so we know in Great Britain or the United States or Germany that it is our problem and our future at stake when a child is starving in Africa or working in a factory in Asia or being recruited at age ten into an army in Central America or denied health care in the United States.

May we see that we have been a species which has not taken seriously the reality that our long-term survival depends upon the care of our young. When a child is battered or a child resorts to gunfire to right some perceived wrong, the community bears a responsibility. Let us ask why we allow advertising money to dictate the programming of violence on TV. Why do we cry lack of money when night basketball courts or other places that give teens a safe gathering spot are closed while bombers and professional sports stadiums continue to be built? Why can we not have a society that helps parents realize the preciousness of the children they bring into this world and offers the support they need to raise our future world citizens to a healthy adulthood in body and mind and spirit?

But help us also know that children are, in some sense, possessions. They belong to all of the human family, and all of the human family is responsible to see that our human species is maintained through conscious care of our progeny. Hear my dream! I dream that those living in the new millennium may come to realize the wisdom of the Native American question, "How does what I am doing today affect the seventh generation?" Help me live my belief that believing in and working for the seventh generation is the only way to make the new millennium a better time for the human species and its environment. Help us know you, Spirit of human wisdom.

Rev. Betty Pingel
Unitarian Universalist minister, Colorado

* * *

Everywhere, true elders will appear within the human community. Neighborhood by neighborhood, they will build bridges across the chasms of ignorance and intolerance that separate us. Thus they will take their rightful place among the young and once again define the terms of the passage into adulthood. The children will be given a way to reach adulthood and the spirit of nature will be enriched by a fully human maturity. The ancient dreams of those who have gone before will be empowered in the councils with such visionary insight that the people will survive. So be it.

Steven Foster
Co-director, The School of Lost Borders, California

You may think
I am a shadow,
But inside
I am a sun.

Damia Gates
Grade 4, Allendale Elementary School, California

✳   ✳   ✳

We do as we do, we say, "for the sake of the future" or "to make a better future for our children." How we can hope to make a good future by doing badly in the present, we do not say. We cannot think about the future, of course, for the future does not exist: the existence of the future is an article of faith. We can be assured only that, if there is to be a future, the good of it is already implicit in the good things of the present. We do not need to plan or devise a "world of the future": if we take care of the world of the present, the future will have received full justice from us. A good future is implicit in the soils, forests, grasslands, marshes, deserts, mountains, rivers, lakes, and oceans that we have now, and in the good things of human culture that we have now; the only valid "futurology" available to us is to take care of those things. We have no need to contrive and dabble at "the future of the human race"; we have the same pressing need that we have always had—to love, care for, and teach our children.

Wendell Berry
Poet, teacher, and farmer, Kentucky

For the Children

Dear Children of the Future.

My hopes for you are these:

May you be Powerfully Loving and Lovingly Powerful. May Love be your Guide with family, friends, and colleagues. Remember to listen carefully to your own Heart and to the Hearts of Others.

May you have the Strength to overcome Fear and Pride and instead follow what has Heart and Meaning for you. Take an Action every day to support your Life Dream, your Love Nature, and your Integrity.

May you care for Mother Nature and the Wilderness and help all living things keep their Dignity.

May you be an active, committed Positive Force in your community. May you show respect to People of All Ages and Races and help make a better world for the Poor, the Sick, the Elderly, and the Youth.

May you respect all the ways human beings access their own Spirituality.

May you constantly bring your Gifts and Talents forward every day without hesitation or reservation.

With deep gratitude and respect for all that you will do to make the Earth a better place in which to live.

Angeles Arrien
Cultural anthropologist, California

The infant's delicate forehead a beacon of promise,
his perfect human face, all that we are
depends on him, his stare from another world,
his great, unblinking eyes so new to earth.

The miraculous one keeps rising among us.
Now do we turn and rush to prepare the way.

Anthony Piccione
Crow Hill Farm, New York

166

*   *   *

Rushing river of days,
Cradle every parent's child in your waters.

We launch our babes in fragile baskets,
Moses multiplied by millions, released from muddy shores.

We squint to see around your bends
As our hearts are carried away.
We toss small sticks to float behind the baskets, our prayers.

Rev. Meg Riley
Director, Unitarian Universalist Association,
Washington, D.C., Office

For the Children

One day we will see God
The Almighty, The Creator
In every child
And perhaps discipline the child
As we wish to be disciplined
And forgive the child
As we wish to be forgiven
And love the child
As we wish to be loved
And uplift the child
As we wish to be uplifted
And teach the child
As we wish to be taught
For one day we will understand, we will know
the Child is God recreated
And God is the Child manifested in flesh
One day we will see God
The Magnificent, The Beautiful
In every child.

167

Sonsyrea Tate
Author and educator, Maryland

We pray for kids on city streets—
    even when they rob us.
We pray for purity in teenagers—
    even when they seduce each other.
We pray for children who could be learning—
    even when they sit in class like zombies.
We pray for the goodness that is buried in young druggies—
    even when they are hustling people.
We pray for them all in the name of the light
    that shines in the darkness—because
    we know that darkness cannot put it out.
We pray for them all in the name of the light
    that lights everyone who comes into the world.
We pray for them all in the name of the light who
    gives us the substance of things hoped for
    and is the evidence of things not seen.

Tony Campolo
Professor of Sociology, Eastern College, Pennsylvania

In this age of change, newness is not what we best offer to the people of the next millennium. Our greatest gifts will be pieces of the past that we shepherd through boundless transition. These are moorings of stability amid constant tumult: durable old ideas, ancient cultures, bastions of wild nature.

The marvel and inspiration to our great-grandkids will not be the latest electronic thinker or space machine. It will be the wondrous products of the slow and the timeless—of evolution itself. Heritage and legacy, in their most basic natural forms, are in serious question. Let us find ways to steward the continuation of places where nature works well enough to produce clean streams, old trees, unique creatures, and fierce predators in their natural balance.

The value of such places will be immeasurable to our descendants and may be the standard by which we are judged.

Mitch Friedman
Environmentalist, Northwest Ecosystem Alliance,
Washington State

I pray that all people of the world will start learning to love each other again. It is time to let go of our hate and put God, love, and respect into our hearts. Let us let go of yesterday and look to the future.

We do not want our grandchildren and their children living in the kind of world we are living in now. All they are learning today is hate. That hate is making their world very small and ugly. That is why so many of our young people are taking their own lives. They deserve a loving world, like the world I knew when I was growing up.

When our Grandfather put us on this earth, he told us to love one another. He didn't say we should hate. It is up to us Elders to stop teaching our young people how to hate. We are their leaders and we must return to the old ways and teach them how to love.

I hope these words will find a place in your hearts.

O'wa'ahta

Marie Smith Jones
Chief of the Eyak Nation, Alaska

Never have we exposed children so early and relentlessly to cultural messages glamorizing violence, sex, possessions, alcohol, and tobacco with so few mediating influences from responsible adults. Never have we experienced such a numbing and reckless reliance on violence to solve problems, feel powerful, or be entertained. Never have so many children been permitted to rely on guns and gangs rather than on parents, neighbors, religious congregations, and schools for protection and guidance. Never have we pushed so many children on to the tumultuous sea of life without the life vests of nurturing families and communities, caring schools, challenged minds, job prospects, and hope.

Never before have we subjected our children to the tyranny of drugs and guns and things or taught them to look for meaning outside rather than inside themselves, teaching them in Dr. King's words "to judge success by the value of our salaries or the size of our automobiles, rather than by the quality of our service and relationships to humanity."

As we face a new century and a new millennium, the overarching challenge for America is to rebuild a sense of community and hope and civility and caring and safety for all our children. I hope God will guide our feet as parents—and guide America's feet—to reclaim our nation's soul, and to give back to all of our children their sense of security and their ability to dream about and work toward a future that is attainable and hopeful.

Marian Wright Edelman
President, Children's Defense Fund, Washington, D.C.

172

Do you think that
the river flows,
because someone says:
"River flow now"?
Do you think that
the elements do
what they are supposed to do
and not what they want to
    do?
If you think so,
then you will never see
and understand what I mean
when I say,
I will be free!

I want to be
free
like a river—
uncontrollable and wild.
I want to be fast and
    dangerous
like the rapids and currents
in the river.
I want to be
like a river
with its different
shades and colors.
I want to be
natural
like a river
in its savagery.

Nadja Awad
Age 15, Sana'a International School,
Yemen

For the Children

I don't thank my creator for creating me. I've discovered that whoever "he" is, he has given life to all of us for a reason. It might be a mission, like he sent Benjamin Franklin to discover electricity. Or it might be someone sent to help a small boy who cannot get his prize out of a gumball machine that needs pounding.

Whoever we are, we've come to walk the face of the Earth for a reason. We all do things that people consider bad or good; whatever quality they have, they still have a place in the circle that weaves around lessons.

There will never be a time when there won't be falsehood and sinning in the world. We can expect all of that in the new millennium. But no matter how bad things are, they still are part of everyday life, and once they happen, you can't do anything about them.

Then again, maybe they teach us things. A house burned down teaches us to be grateful for a roof. Violations of any kind teach us to be more respectful of all things.

We've all come here for a reason. Whatever our purpose is, we've got to free it. My prayer for the future is that we make better use of our time together on this Earth as united human beings.

Phoebe Ann Jones
Age 11, Costa Rica

O Ruler of all, our sure defense, we pray for the world our children live in and will inherit.

Have pity on us, O Lord.

For the sake of all children, bring an end to the buildup and proliferation of nuclear and other weapons. Preserve us from attitudes and acts that threaten the annihilation of all life and the future we hold in trust for the children.

We cry to You, Creator of all.

For the sake of all children, bring an end to conflict and war between nations. Give us hearts and minds of peace and help us to teach peace to our children.

We cry to You, Creator of all.

For the sake of all children, bring an end to our misuse and pollution of the land, air, and water of the Earth. Teach us to be stewards and guardians of Your creation.

We cry to You, Creator of all.

For the sake of all children, bring an end to the injustices caused and abetted by those in places of power. May our hearts and minds be changed by the cries of Your hungry and suffering children.

We cry to You, Creator of all.

O Holy God, through whom all things are transformed and made whole, grant us and our children newness of life. Refresh and sustain us with the glorious vision of Your world to come, in which all children will live in peace and harmony, all children will be filled with good things to eat, and all children will rest secure in Your love.

O God Most High, whom we name Yahweh, Lord, and Our Father, Creator, Redeemer, and Sanctifier of the world, we ask these things on behalf of our children and generations yet unborn who will live to praise Your Holy Name, world without end.
Amen.

> *Written by the Children's Defense Fund*
> *for National Children's Day, June 1982,*
> *Washington, D.C.*

*   *   *

Keep your heart clean with peace. Don't get it dirty with greed. It is not too late to clean it.

> *Kaila Spencer*
> *Age 8, Friends' School, Colorado*

*   *   *

Let's use this moment
To leap beyond our fear
Landing upright on earth
Among the wildflowers.

> *Naomi Mattis*
> *Buddhist teacher and counselor, New Mexico*

For the Children

Everybody is talking about youth.
Who is listening to us?

A.J.D.
Age 19, from a speech delivered at a WP2N Conference at the
United Nations

*   *   *

The problem in my country is war and malnutrition. My parents and my brothers were killed in the war. I joined the forces when I was twelve because I was told I would have food and should take revenge on the death of my parents. Please don't be afraid of me. I am not a soldier anymore. I am just a child. And what I want to say is that people fight because they think they can take revenge. But there is no revenge. You kill and you kill, but it will never stop. There is no such thing as revenge.

Ishmael Beah
Age 15, Sierra Leone (as told to Laura Simms)

*   *   *

One day during a storm a heavy branch fell onto a little snowdrop plant. Later when the branch was removed the small tender stems, unharmed, were seen to have spread out and curled around as if to embrace the log. Less than an hour later, the little shoots had all but straightened out and, unimpeded, were growing upward toward their fulfillment.

Murshida Sitara Brutnell
The Sufi Way, England

For the Children

grandmother
you were silenced before you could
finish telling me the stories
i am coming home
i am listening everywhere
for your voice

Jeanetta Calhoun
Poet

*   *   *

The clock struck midnight and a new millennium began. Grandmother Time, all wrinkled and folded in wisdom, nodded and smiled. "How long is a thousand years?" you ask her. "Let me tell you," she answered, "it's only as long as the blink of an eye or maybe as quick as a heartbeat. It's as short as a sneeze or the snap of your fingers. It's a mere moment in the Mystery."

"But let me tell you this as well. When you love instead of kill, time grows long. When you preserve and create instead of use and destroy, time grows full. And when you give yourself to time, yes, when you open yourself to each moment—not avoiding either suffering or joy—then time is no time. Then time is forever time. Then you will be a stranger to nothing and to no one. Then time will turn your shimmering and fleeting life into love. You will be part of the Mystery that does not cease."

Gunilla Norris
Psychotherapist, Connecticut

178

Please bring strange things.
Please come bringing new things.
Let very old things come into your hands.
Let what you do not know come into your eyes.
Let desert sand harden your feet.
Let the arch of your feet be the mountains.
Let the paths of your fingertips be your maps
and the ways you go be the lines on your palms.
Let there be deep snow in your inbreathing
and your outbreath be the shining of ice.
May your mouth contain the shapes of strange words.
May you smell food cooking you have not eaten.
May the spring of a foreign river be your navel.
May your soul be at home where there are no houses.
Walk carefully, well-loved one,
walk mindfully, well-loved one,
walk fearlessly, well-loved one.
Return with us, return to us,
be always coming home.

Ursula K. Le Guin
Author, Pennsylvania

For the Children

Whose blood runs the rivers of the world? Whose breath sings the sorrow of the universe? In the eye of the enemy, can you see your own soul? When a baby cries in the outcasts' camp, do you long to hold her? Can you comfort & soothe & rock her like the rhythm of the waters of the world?

all children
are our
children

179

may we embrace all human bodies.
may we not collapse in our suffering.
may we yearn to comfort & share the sacred.
may we celebrate all ways of worship.
may we throw back our heads in wide human laughter.
let the colors & the fear mingle & disperse.
all rivers are blood rivers. all blood is all blood &

every child
is our
precious child.

Michelle T. Clinton and Rev. G. Collette Jackson
California

For the Children

Remember the sky that you were born under,
know each of the star's stories.
Remember the moon, know who she is.
Remember the sun's birth at dawn, that is the
strongest point of time. Remember sundown
and the giving away to night.
Remember your birth, how your mother struggled
to give you form and breath. You are evidence of
her life, and her mother's, and hers.
Remember your father. He is your life, also.
Remember the earth whose skin you are:
red earth, black earth, yellow earth, white earth
brown earth, we are earth.
Remember the plants, trees, animal life who all have their
tribes, their families, their histories, too. Talk to them,
listen to them. They are alive poems.
Remember the wind. Remember her voice.
She knows the origin of this universe.
Remember that you are all people
and that all people are you.
Remember that you are this universe
and that this universe is you.
Remember that all is in motion, is growing, is you.
Remember that language comes from this.
Remember the dance that language is, that life is.
Remember.

Joy Harjo
Poet and editor, Muskogee Nation, New Mexico

For the Children

The mud shall cover our sins
and the water shall wash us free
and the brush shall cleanse our skin
and the wind shall weave our hair
and the sun shall bless our face.
The sky shall clothe us in blue.

181

Nicole Thibodeaux
Grade 10, Taos High School, New Mexico

* * *

In the next century
or the one beyond that
they say,
are valleys, pastures.
We can meet there in peace
if we make it.
To climb these coming crests
one word to you, to
you and your children:
stay together
learn the flowers
go light.

Gary Snyder
Poet, California

For the Children

THIS HOLY EARTH

The earth is a sacred reality. The voices in Part 6 speak of the immanence of spirit in the natural world. Every notion we have of the divine has been shaped by our experience of this planet. If we have a wonderful sense of the divine, it is because we live amid such beauty. As the Passionist priest and philosopher Thomas Berry observes, "If we lived on the moon, our mind and emotions, our speech, our imagination, our sense of the divine would all reflect the desolation of the lunar landscape." Clearly the earth is our primary revelatory environment. Our most sacred scripture is the "holy book" of nature.

While the distinction between spirit and matter is valid, the two are inseparable. Spirit and matter are not two different realms of reality, two different layers of the universe. The same reality will be material or spiritual depending on how we approach it. No matter where we immerse ourselves in the stream of reality, we can touch the spiritual source of all that is natural.

Until recently, the holiness of the earth has been largely forgotten in most modern industrial cultures. Under the worldview of secular materialism, the land became mere real estate, and the animals and trees simply resources to be used for our benefit. In pursuing this utilitarian and commercial relationship, we have destroyed places of more beauty and diverse life than we will ever be able to recreate. However, this attitude toward the earth has begun to change, as the prayers in Part 6 witness. Increasingly around the world, people are expressing their determination to protect and restore the beauty of the earth and the diversity of its life. The madness of the destruction has come home to us. "To commit a crime against the natural world is a sin," declared His Holiness Bartholomew I, Archbishop of Constantinople and New Rome, in 1998. This statement was greeted as an unprecedented defense of the environment by the religious leader of a major international church. But the Greek Orthodox patriarch does not stand alone in recognizing that environmental abuse must stop. His voice is joined by millions of others—among them the poets, priests, ministers, teachers, and activists in Part 6—calling for healing. As the environmentalist Stephanie Mills writes:

> The sacred in Nature is finding a voice audible and intelligible to our moment. We can grow whole in an emulation of Nature's disinterested generosity. It is our restoration to a timeless understanding, an immense knowledge; now a new era can begin.

This is an inspiring vision: that our deepening recognition of the sacred in nature is opening us to "an immense knowledge" that will guide us in the centuries to come. Surely we will not continue the myopic pursuit of even more economic growth based on the depletion of the earth's treasures. To build a sustainable society that recognizes the sacred in nature, we must come to terms with limits, however much that disturbs the outdated goals of political and business leaders. As we acknowledge our ecological limits, we will be freed to create lives of nobility rather than greed. The prayers that follow give us glimpses of this freedom and of the reverence we may know as we walk this holy earth.

They say there will be new heavens then, and a new earth. And I say, these old ones are good enough. They've been around for hardly more than a blink of an eye. They're certainly not old enough to just throw them away. Or even wish them away. I know we get tired of the pain sometimes, of the sweat and of our own frailness. But I swear I've seen angels cry from envy because we can walk barefoot in grass. This place is good, glorious, and, I believe, ultimately forgiving. We've been foolish, small-minded, cruel even, but dear sweet earth keeps composting everything, even our sins. Red worms and vultures are our best confessors, and in the end we will be converted to their true faith. Probably all of this is illusion, but in the meantime, earth is beautiful and solid beneath us, and sun and moon and rain and stars and wind are blessing us. If we will only learn to receive life's smile, and give it back through our very pores, it will all be okay. I'm sure of it.

187

Mary Vineyard
Massage therapist, New Mexico

We seek a renewed stirring of love for the Earth. We plead that what we are capable of doing to it is often what we ought not to do. We urge that all people now determine that an untrammeled wilderness shall remain here to testify that this generation had love for the next. We would celebrate a new renaissance. The old one found a way to exploit. The new one has discovered the Earth's limits. Knowing those limits, we may learn anew what compassion and beauty are, and pause to listen to the Earth's music. We may see that progress is neither the accelerating speed with which we multiply and subdue the Earth nor the growing number of things we possess and cling to. It is a way along which to search for truth, to find serenity and love and reverence for life, to be part of an enduring harmony, trying hard not to sing out of tune.

David Brower
Founder, Earth Island Institute, California

The sound of the drum
is held in each heart.
Pakholigan, dzidzis, nigawes. *
We heard its music
long before breath or vision.
Its beat is the pulse of an ancient sea.
I summon its rhythm to carry this prayer.

189

As our unshod feet
caress mother earth
let us feel that same tempo,
that old affirmation
that no borders exist
between breath and breath,
no lines drawn on paper
can restrain the dawn.

Let us all now remember
that first lullaby
we danced before birth
that beat of first life,
that great tide of first peace.

Like the wings of the eagle
thrumming the wind
let our song carry wide
between earth and sky.

Joseph Bruchac
Poet and author, Abenaki Nation, New York

---

* These are the Abenaki words for *drum, baby, mother.*

This Holy Earth

We have a beautiful
mother
Her hills
are buffaloes
Her buffaloes
hills.

We have a beautiful
mother
Her oceans
are wombs
Her wombs
oceans.

We have a beautiful
mother
Her teeth

the white stones
at the edge
of the water
the summer grasses
her plentiful
hair.

We have a beautiful
mother
Her green lap
immense
Her brown embrace
eternal
Her blue body
everything
we know.

Alice Walker
Author, California

This Holy Earth

We believe in the one message
like a fever chill
in each mushroom, inside
the chanterelle, the morel,
the rose coral and shaggy mane.
We believe plankton travel the sea's veins.
We believe the towhee.
We believe alpine snow water, when it teases the crags
and outcrops like clear crystal,
is memorizing sunlight to help the oysters grow.
We believe in synchronicity. We believe when a poem is
    conceived
the beloved knows. We believe Jupiter touches us with luck
as we live and live again, and that Jesus knew.
We believe sod holds. We believe there are
in each of us particles that once
were stars, that matter is thought,
and that this belief is the way
of breathing in.

James Bertolino
Visiting professor, Creative Writing,
Willamette University, Oregon

In the name of every muscle in our bodies, we beseech you
In the name of the feather, the sun, the mountain, the river,
the otter, the salmon, the pine and the stone
In the name of babies, now and forever more,
and of lovers, and of sex.
In the name of the breathing, pushing, spreading, decaying,
pulsing earth beneath our gills, our roots, our talons, our
hooves and our bare-skinned feet:

Help us.
Help us easily distracted, heartbreakingly self-centered,
brilliant and beautiful big-brained creatures,
Us business-as-usual, new-on-the-planet, slow-moving, deep-
loving creatures
Help us to remember that this wondrously intelligent orb has
generated living art beyond anything we will ever hope to
approximate
Twenty-four hours a day
For six billion years—

Help us to remember that we can seize the power
That we can raise our voices
That we can flood the courtrooms, the schoolrooms, the
boardrooms,
the email, the voicemail, letters to the editor, the streets,
the banks, the churches, and the temples
That we can rise up in power on behalf of all those who live
in tree, cave, hive, village, river, ocean and suburb.
That we can rise up on behalf of all we love and all that keeps
us alive.

This Holy Earth

We beseech you: visible and invisible,
wild and tame, past, present and future.
Have mercy on us human beings.
Help us give birth to the human race.

Libby Roderick
Singer and composer, Turtle Island Records, Alaska

193

This Holy Earth

O Sacred Source, the One of no names and all names, my journey back to you is the source of my unity with all others, and I give thanks. I weave my gratitude into the memory of these moments which have shaped my inner and outer being. I give thanks for the present moment and for the Story by which my eyes can see and my ears can hear what you have revealed in the shaping of the Universe. I give you thanks for the Story by which I know the fifteen billion years of my unfolding.

I give you thanks for the enormous contribution of those who
    lived before me,
for the thousands of years during which humans crafted their
    images of you in the image of the feminine and of the
    Earth,
for loosening our tongues that we might utter words about
    your eternal word,
for the Ice Ages that shaped the lands, mountains, and rivers,
    that have in turn shaped our imaginations,
for all of the mammals who have taught us to birth and suc-
    cor our young,
for the coming of the flowering plants that channel their en-
    ergy into the seeds by which the future is endowed,
for the birds who brought song and melody to the Earth,
for the great green plants and their interdependence with in-
    sects,
for all the teeming life within the oceans which fashioned the
    sensing organs of Earth,
for the first simple life forms that learned to take nourishment
    from the sun, our mother star, and laid down a pattern of

This Holy Earth

giving themselves away to others, and receiving life from others,

for the super nova event by which our mother star collapsed and created the stardust out of which this solar system was formed,

for stars and galaxies in which is incarnated all the dreams, visions, and energies by which you have shaped this present moment,

for the first moment—that utter act of giving by which you brought forth this single body of the universe out of which I weave the web of my own existence

for the dark, impenetrable, pregnant, awesome mystery that you are, and out of which you called my name.

Amen.

Sr. Miriam MacGillis
Genesis Farm, New Jersey

Lie quietly along the earth
That sky may send its strength through you
Into the spinning planet.
Absorb from eons of tumultuous change
The rhythms pulsing up through fire and water,
    rock and roots of growing things,
Your body filtering with flesh and spirit
Earth's vibrant offering to the sky.
You are the instrument of peace,
The promise of renewal to a time and place
    not of your body
But dependent on your willingness to give yourself
    to earth and sky;
To make belief in goodness shape a thousand years to come.
May blessings be your gift, both given and received.

Great spirit, father of us all,
Dear mother earth,
Combine your might
And use our love
To make this body whole,
For now and forever.

Judith Billings
Consultant, President's Advisory Council on HIV/AIDS,
Washington State

This Holy Earth

O creation
confiding moon
every possibility is unveiled
the beauty of pearl white
laughing across the cosmos
making lunar landing
upon our
earthen souls
o creation
we are praying
let us mirror
your glorious
your unspeakable
let us
in a good way
the seas the rivers
deer and muskrat
trout and fireflies

that which we cannot ever
let us swell
magnify our hearts
like a gracile crescent
into the full-on lady of love
o creation
we are asking
let us
bowing clasping
knees in the waves
dream this sad century
into a new cycle for life
beauty will laugh
moons
among us
and we will
in a good way
o creation

Chellis Glendinning
Environmentalist and author, New Mexico

Haah-nah'e ma'heo'o, GREAT ONE,
You who bless your entire creation with spiritual life—
> With sacred water,
> With the sacred light and fire of the sun,
> With the sacred sky dome covering of air, and
> With the sacred red earth altar, from where I send out
> my prayers to the four sacred directions.

Ne-a'ese, hear this humble prayer.

I thank you for the Grandfather Spirit Power of the East-Southeast, the place of beginnings.

I pray for the young mother who is bringing new life to the people—bless her and her baby with health and serenity.

I pray for the small child, new to the earth walk on this medicine wheel of earth—bless this new life with all things good and with long life.

I turn in prayer to the Grandfather Spirit Power of the South-Southwest, the place of continued human growth called youth.

I pray for the young person, both male and female—bless this person with power and awareness to walk as a respectful relative to earth and everything on and in it.

I turn in prayer to the Grandfather Spirit Power of the West-Northwest, the place of adulthood.

I pray for a man and a woman, the humble, two-legged walker with five fingers.

Bless this person, this parent, this grandparent with spiritual knowledge and patience to build a good, stable family and a strong, unified community.

This Holy Earth

I turn my prayer to the Grandfather Spirit Power of the North-Northwest, the place of wisdom and old age.

I pray for the elder that has walked long on this earth and experienced the wonder and mystery of life.

Bless this beloved grandparent with a generous heart and spirit to wisely and lovingly share the sacred teachings of life.

I turn back to the East and pray that all my relatives be clothed with holiness, with *ma'heo'ne-vestse*.

Ma'heo'ne-vestse all those yet to be born.

Ma'heo'ne-vestse animal people, water people.

Ma'heo'ne-vestse crawling people, flying people.

Ma'heo'ne-vestse rooted people.

Ma'heo'ne-vestse human beings,

Who too are spiritually rooted in the good Mother Earth,

Who must collectively be prayerful-minded about the sacredness and interdependence of life.

Bless us with the knowledge and wisdom to live as good relatives, with happy hearts and strong spirits, who can face the next millennium with the courage of love and power of peace.

Hena'haanehe.

Henrietta Mann
Cheyenne, professor of Native American Studies,
University of Montana

This Holy Earth

May we wake to the new millennium as waking from a troubled dream to a morning boding fair. May we recognize and turn away from the dark forces, inner and outer, that for so long have manipulated us and mangled our incomparable home planet. May the healing energy be unfurled.

May our senses reawaken to the inexpressible beauty of each other, the living world, and the universe beyond. May we come to know all life, from blade of grass to human child to mountain range, as interconnected, interacting, and inseparable over all the Earth, throughout all the time that is allotted to us.

Nancy Jack Todd
Editor, Annals of Earth, Massachusetts

Great Mother Wisdom, you are the sustaining source of life and renewal of life. We forgot you; we lost touch with you, as we fled into our own minds and climbed our own hierarchies, seeking to make God in the image of our fantasies of domination over the earth, over conquered land, animals, and people. Now our folly is turning to ashes in our mouth. Our power, which we trusted to make us immortal, disconnected from body, from earth, returns to us as toxic waste and acid rain. We seek your healing touch, your nourishing presence. O Mother Wisdom, it is you on whose bosom all things lie; from your womb all things well up as from an infinite font of life. Into you all things return, falling into their many parts, to rise again from your fertile matrix as new growth, new plants, new animals.

You are ongoing life that sustains this wondrous cycle of birth and death and rebirth. Can we learn once more to live in harmony with your ways, imitating forests and meadows that make no poisons? Our proud cities, alienated from your truth, threaten to collapse like a house of cards; nay, not so easily. How many innocent lives of birds, butterflies, furry beasts, creeping things, flying things, and swimming things will be taken down with us in our demise? Let us quiet our madness and listen to your still voice, feel your warmth pushing up between the cracks of our concrete pavements. Claim us, your erring offspring, as your own, before it is too late.

Rosemary Radford Ruether
Author and professor, Garrett Evangelical Seminary, Illinois

And the voice of God comes to us,
    as it came to Moses long ago by a burning bush:
    "Take off your shoes;
    the earth on which you stand is holy ground,
    for I have hallowed it with my care and compassion
    since time began."

202

Forgive us, O God, when we have eyes and do not see the
    beauty of your creation;
Forgive us, O God, when we have ears and do not hear the
    wondrous music of heavenly spheres,
    not to mention the birds beneath our own windows.
Forgive us our poverty of the senses;
    and the shallowness of our sense of awe;
    and our misunderstanding of value as we put dollar signs
    on your other species, even as we destroy them.

Your whole universe, O God, O Creator, is a burning bush.
It calls us to turn aside, to pay attention,
    to see and hear and sense—and to wonder and to praise.
Grant us new eyes, new ears, and newly awakened hearts;
    to enter into your courts of nature
    and praise your holy presence here.

Elizabeth Dodson Gray
Author, Massachusetts

This Holy Earth

I came off Bear Peak, the quick descent through Fern
    Canyon.
Forest Service signs, tacked onto fir trees, alert literate
    humans
to raptor birds nested in overhead cliffs.
Waiting for my companion, perched on a wayside boulder,
I listened to bird song. Three or four times thunder cracked
down the ravine, trail winding and twisting through cloud
    back to Bear Peak.
Lower down, gold sun filtered by pines; and fresh rain.
Walking again, my thought turned to
Vimalakirti—old India lay buddha—who gave discourse on
    emptiness
to humans, devas, garuda birds, animals, ghosts, gandharvas,
    dancing girls,
by the thousands—all fitting elbow to elbow, no problem,
not even a jostling, into his bamboo studio. Sweet taste of
    Dharma
not for humans alone. It was then I dropped
into a fern and wildflower gulch, fantastically pungent with
odor of mammal. I knew
who to watch for.

203

> Room for you too
>   O black bear
>   in Vimalakirti's ten-foot cell.

Andrew Schelling
"Haibun Ursus Americanus"
Poet, Professor of Writing and Poetics,
The Naropa Institute, Colorado

This Holy Earth

Return blessings, O Holy Ones,
    So life's cycles can continue with beauty, balance, and
        abundance.
    May life's cycles return blessings.

Return blessings, Sacred Earth,
    So air, water, fire, and food can nourish all we hold dear.
    May air, water, fire, and food return blessings.

Return blessings, Beloved Sisters and Brothers,
    So all creation can share pleasure and do justice.
    May all creation return blessings.

Return blessings, Crawling Creatures and Winged Friends,
    So the earth can be renewed.
    May the earth return blessings.

Return blessings, Trees, Flowers, Rivers, Mountains,
    So nature can refresh our spirits.
    May nature return blessings.

Return blessings, Stars, Moons, Planets, Galaxies,
    So wonder can nourish our visions.
    May wonder return blessings.

Return blessings, Changing Seasons,
    So life's cycles can end in peace.
    May life's cycles return blessings.

Diann L. Neu
Co-director, The Women's Alliance for
Theology, Ethics, and Ritual (WATER), Maryland

This Holy Earth

The earth is a living, conscious being. In company with cultures of many different times and places, we name these things as sacred: air, fire, water, and earth.

Whether we see them as the breath, energy, blood, and body of the Mother, or as the blessed gifts of a Creator, or as symbols of the interconnected systems that sustain life, we know that nothing can live without them.

To call these things sacred is to say that they have a value beyond their usefulness for human ends, that they themselves become the standards by which our acts, our economics, our laws, and our purposes must be judged. No one has the right to appropriate them or profit from them at the expense of others. Any government that fails to protect them forfeits its legitimacy.

All people, all living things, are part of the earth's life, and thus are sacred. No one of us stands higher or lower than any other. Only justice can assure balance; only ecological balance can sustain freedom. Only in freedom can that fifth sacred thing we call *spirit* flourish in its full diversity.

To honor the sacred is to create conditions in which nourishment, sustenance, habitat, knowledge, freedom, and beauty can thrive. To honor the sacred is to make love possible.

To this we dedicate our curiosity, our will, our courage, our silences, and our voices. To this we dedicate our lives.

Starhawk
Author and teacher, California

This Holy Earth

The moon is angry
because you are afraid of the dark

because you have forgotten to praise the stately dimensions of
    the dark
neglected the shrines and let the stones of the altars fall down

because you don't remember the words for darkness
because your mother and father failed to practice the move-
    ment
and to teach you the steps and the notes
because your mother and father failed to keep the air over the
    altars pure

because you have constructed dry places
where the temples of trees stood
and permitted cement in the clearings
where fairy rings spread their expanding circle of spore

and because you fill darkness with revolving searchlights
because you fill darkness with the jangle of money
because you fill darkness with the blat of machinery
because you fill darkness with the tinny babble of your
    nervousness

because you no longer run at dawn
because you don't know how to sit still at dusk
because you shrink from each other's darkness
that sheath over the fiery central core

because you have not once visited the cathedrals of the dark
and worshiped there in silence

This Holy Earth

and because you no longer have the dignity to atone for these
    things
the moon stops the fountain of your sleep
and drives you out   wide awake and burning
to wander and pace   mouth dry eyes burning

so that you are forced to acknowledge your own body
and to remember the body is holy
and to remember this body is one body
and this earth the one holy body you cannot desecrate with
    impunity

so that you understand that if you deny the dark
you make a mockery of light.

Marilyn Krysl
"Why You Can't Sleep"
Poet, Colorado

208

Kindler and rekindler
of universes, the fire burns forever.
It is the flame of life that courses through
all generations from first to last,
that burns without consuming,
that is itself consumed and renewed
inexhaustibly, life after life,
generation after generation,
species after species,
galaxy after galaxy,
universe after universe,
each sharing in the blaze for its season
and going down to death while
the fire burns on undiminished.
The fire is life itself,
the life of this universe,
of this galaxy, of this planet,
of this place and every place:
the place by the rock
and the place under the hill
and the place by the river
and the place in the forest,
no two alike anywhere.
And the life of every place is god,
who is the fire:
the life of the pond, god;
the life of the tundra, god;
the life of the sea, god;
the life of the land, god;
the life of the earth, god;

This Holy Earth

the life of the universe, god;
in every place unique,
as the life of every place is unique,
and in every place the same,
as the fire that burns is everywhere
THE FIRE OF LIFE.

Daniel Quinn
Author, Texas

*　　*　　*

We look at our reflections each morning for a thousand
　　years
to see our eyes as those of tigers
taking back the Tiger Earth, of whales
returning to the Whale Sea, of hawks circling
on Hawk Air, and for a moment each day
we recognize the fur beneath our skin,
the feathers beneath the fur, and the scales
beneath the feathers.
We walk backward through a forest of machines
until there is space to place an ear to the ground
and listen to the grinding of roots
as they, like us, work their way to water
clear enough for us to see the possibility
of time as our friend.

David Chorlton
Poet and editor, Arizona

This Holy Earth

I love the Mother Earth
as much as (almost more
than) my own mother
and my mother's mother—
the Earth who is my mother
as really as any mother
I ever had. The Mother Earth
whose name is Estelle Poniewaz
and a billion other names
and who is a zillion living
beings who have no name,
untaxonomied by all the
taxidermists who ever
taxed the lineages
of nonhuman beings that
ever emerged like me
from this vast Mother of an Earth
made love to by the Father Sun.

I love the Mother Earth
even more than the Virgin Mother
(Hail Mary of whose womb
blessed was the fruit).
I love the Mother Earth,
this dear old granny of a planet
this greatgreatgreatgreat
grandgrandgrandgrand Mother
of a living breathing planet
whose breaths are the clouds
more than I love Jesus Mary Joseph

This Holy Earth

put together, with the Holy Ghost
thrown in for good measure.

I love the Mother Earth
more than Jesus Moses Buddha
Mohammed Krishna and all those
other definitely lovable folks
put together. This Mother
Earth from whose sacred womb
I sprang so many years ago—
and from whom also sprang
all my myriad brothers &
sisters, human & non- :
two-legged, four-legged,
wing'd, finn'd, whatever.

211

Happy Mother's Day
dear tormented Mother,
more full of sorrows than
the Sorrowful Mother
of crucified Humankind.
Forgive your six billion
ungrateful brats, so many children
she didn't know what to do,
her children eating her
out of house and home.
Happy Earth Day/ReBirth Day,
teach us your wisdom
that we and you may live.

Jeff Poniewaz
Poet, Wisconsin

This Holy Earth

This we believe:

Humans have become so numerous and our tools so powerful
  that we have driven fellow creatures to extinction,
    dammed the great rivers,
  torn down ancient forests, poisoned the earth, rain and
    wind,
  and ripped holes in the sky.

Our science has brought pain as well as joy;
  our comfort is paid for by the suffering of millions.

We are learning from our mistakes, we are mourning our
  vanished kin,
  and we now build a new politics of hope.

We respect and uphold the absolute need for clean air, water,
  and soil.

We see that economic activities that benefit the few
  while shrinking the inheritance of many are wrong.

And since environmental degradation erodes biological
  capital forever,
  full ecological and social cost must enter all equations of
  development.

We are one brief generation in the long march of time;
  the future is not ours to erase.

So where knowledge is limited, we will remember all those who
  will walk after us, and err on the side of caution.

David Suzuki
The David Suzuki Foundation, Canada

Listen, my children. The Spirit who moved over the dry land is not pleased. I am thirsty. Are you listening?

We are listening, Mother Earth. Speak.

The Spirit who filled the waters is not pleased. I choke with debris and pollution. Are you listening?

The Spirit who brought beauty to the Earth is not pleased. The Earth grows ugly with misuse. Are you listening?

The Spirit who brought forth all the creatures is being destroyed. Are you listening?

The Spirit who gave humans life and a path to walk together is not pleased. You are losing your humanity, and your footsteps stray from the path. Are you listening?

Let us pray. O God, you created the Earth in goodness and in beauty. Forgive all that we have done to harm the Earth. O God, you have filled the Earth with food for our sustenance. Forgive us for not sharing the gifts of the Earth. You have created us, O God, of one blood throughout the Earth. Forgive us for not living as sisters and brothers should.

Sr. Mary Rosita Shiosse, S.B.S.

If I could wish the total and complete restoration of the world and the banishing of despair, I would wish for the immediate preservation of all species, all prairies, all forests, all swamps, all deserts; and for a return of crazy love, of go-for-broke passion between women and men, women and women, men and men, human beings of all ages and places; between humans and the soil and everything that arises therefrom. Let the love and commitment between beings be part of this great healing. If only we can dare to belong to one another and to the land!

If we can approach our particular life-place humbly, attentively, openly, and with hopeful anticipation; if we earnestly try to discern what that place has wanted to be, what ecological community it has given rise to; if we try to be of real service to our life-places, we will see healing and we will know love again. Conceivably, the good feeling engendered within the Earth community as restoration gains ground and beauty returns could spiral wildly out of control and joy prevail.

The sacred in nature is finding a voice audible and intelligible to our moment. We can grow whole in an emulation of Nature's disinterested generosity. It is our restoration to a timeless understanding, an immense knowledge; now a new era can begin. A last chance and a first chance. We go out from the garden and into the wild.

Stephanie Mills
Environmental activist and author, Michigan

In New Jersey once, marigolds grew wild.
Fields swayed with daisies.
Oaks stood tall on mountains.
Powdered butterflies graced the velvet air.

Listen. It was like that.
Before the bulldozers.
Before the cranes.
Before the cement sealed the earth.

Even the stars, which used to hang
in thick clusters in the black sky,
even the stars are dim.

Burrow under the blacktop,
under the cement, the old dark earth
is still there. Dig your hands into it,
feel it, deep, alive on your fingers.

Know that the earth breathes and pulses still.
Listen. It mourns. In New Jersey once,
flowers grew.

Maria Mazziotti Gillan
Poet, New Jersey

To the Winds of the South
Amaru, great serpent, Mother of the Waters
Teach us your ways,
To shed the past the way you shed your skin,
To walk softly on the Earth.
Teach us the Beauty Way.

To the Winds of the West
Mother Jaguar, Otorongo,
Come to us.
Show us the way of the Luminous Warrior
who has no enemies in this world or the next.
Teach us to live impeccably, with integrity.
Show us the ways beyond death.

To the Winds of the North
Royal Hummingbird.
Grandmothers and Grandfathers,
Ancient Ones.
Come and warm your hands by our fires.
Speak to us in the howling wind
And in the crackling of the fire.
We come to honor you who have come before us,
And you who will come after us,
Our children's children.

To the Winds of the East
Great condor, eagle.
Come to us from the place of the rising Sun.
Keep us under your wing,
Take us to the mountains we only dare to dream of.
Teach us to always fly wing to wing with the Great Spirit.

This Holy Earth

Pachamama, Mother Earth
We thank you for your breath, your waters,
For holding us so sweetly.
We've gathered in your name, Mother,
For the healing of all of your children.
The Stone People.
The Plant People.
The four-legged, the two-legged, the creepy crawlers.
The finned, the feathered, the furred.
All Our Relations.

Father Sun, grandmother Moon, to the Star Nations.
Great Spirit, creator of all.
You who are known by a thousand names
And you who are the nameless One.
Thank you for bringing us together
And allowing us to sing the Song of Life.

Alberto Villoldo
Anthropologist and student of the Incas,
Four Winds Society, Florida

This Holy Earth

On that day
the salmon shall return
(whole tribes of them
    swimming together):
giant chinooks, silvers, &
    pinks,
reds & steelhead, quartz-
    nosed leapers:
old tailwalker, mountain-
    climber,
mad for the glaciers;
flooding the rivers, clothing
    the land
in its vast body, healing the
    scars,
and calling us home.

And on that day
the trees shall return
(whole forests of them,
    marching together):
red cedar (the sacred tree),
fir & hemlock,
spruce & pine,
redwood & cypress,
juniper & yew;
cloud-scrapers piercing the
    skies,
bringing down the rains,
holding the earth,
setting the rivers free;

and the mountains shall
    become
fountains of the waters.

And on that day
the animals shall return
(whole flocks & herds of
    them):
eagle & raven, otter &
    beaver,
wren & hummingbird,
coyote & bear, elk & wolf;
and all the lost species
shall pour from the ark:
each to their own home-
    place,
and the woods & waters shall
    sing!

And on that great day
the peoples shall return
(whole communities & na-
    tions):
Our families, friends, &
    neighbors,
all our relations, with
the old ones from the
time before time began . . .

All the people who have ever
lived here will gather
    together

in one great Potlatch to
    remember—
"Give away as you were
    given"—
and the house of names shall
call out and dance again!

And on that sacred day
the spirits shall return:
Grandfather and Grand-
    mother,
the Great Spirit,
southwind and winterwave;
sun, moon, and stars shall
align us here down below;
and the lord of the mountains
and the lord of the sea—Bear
    & Orca—

shall dance long looping
    circles together,
restoring the hoop of the
    world.

And our teachers shall return,
all the great spirits of this
    region,
be here with us now.
All praise and thanks to those
who help us learn
to sing this land, and
find our way home!

On that day . . .
And on that great day . . .
And on that joyous day . . .

219

David D. McCloskey
Teacher and bioregionalist, Cascadia Institute, Washington State

---

This Holy Earth

On the rim of the millennium, I am sitting on the rim of the
    pond
on a summer evening listening to the frogs.

Come with us, we ask.
May we do nothing to diminish your singing.

220

Who said anything about a millennium? Not you.
Croak! A thousand years have passed.

The earth likes your leap and plop
better than our global flights.

You are good company in the evening's moment by the pond,
but below and beyond this pleasure of dusk,

your chorus is important,
and your presence at the watery gates of things,

creation itself passing
through your green body.

May we do nothing to diminish your singing.
Come with us, we ask.

Howard Nelson
Teacher, Cayuga Community College, New York

Our sin toward the world, or the spiritual root of all our pollution, lies in our refusal to view life and the world as a sacrament of thanksgiving and as a gift of constant communion with God on a global scale.

We believe that our first task is to raise the consciousness of adults—those who most use the resources and gifts of the planet. Ultimately, we must perceive our every action as having a direct effect upon the future of the environment. Human beings and the environment form a seamless garment of existence, a complex fabric that we believe is fashioned by God.

We lovingly suggest to all the people of the Earth that they seek to help one another to understand the myriad ways in which we are related to the Earth and to one another. In this way, we may begin to repair the dislocation many people experience in relation to creation.

We must be spokespeople for an ecological ethic that reminds the world that it is not ours to use for our own convenience. It is God's gift of love to us, and we must return his love by protecting it and all that is in it.

The Lord suffuses all of creation with His divine presence in one continuous legato from the substance of atoms to the Mind of God. Let us renew the harmony between Heaven and Earth, and transfigure every detail, every particle of life. Let us love one another—and lovingly learn from one another—for the edification of God's people, for the sanctification of God's creation, and for the glorification of God's most holy Name. Amen.

His All Holiness Ecumenical Patriarch Bartholomew I
The Eastern Orthodox Church

222

Today, now, this moment,
I promise myself to reach out and touch the earth.
I will dig my fingers into the soil and remember what it is that
    sustains me.

> It is not wealth.
> It is not possessions.
> It is not achievements.
> It is not the praise of men.

It is this that I touch, the sacred soil, the fertile field, the
    living land, the holy.

Today, now, this moment,
I promise myself to reach out and touch a fellow creature.
I will run my hand along fur, feathers, shell, or scales and re-
    member what sustains him.

> It is not wealth.
> It is not possessions.
> It is not achievements.
> It is not the praise of men.

It is the ocean eternal, the infinite sky, the sun, the rain, the
    holy earth.

Today, now, this moment.
I promise myself to reach out and embrace understanding.
I will hold to my breast the reality that my fellow creatures
    and I are equals in the Mother's love.

This Holy Earth

It is not wealth.
It is not possessions.
It is not achievements.
It is not the praise of men.

It is food and breath, life and death, the stars above us and the holy earth.

Laurel Olson
Community Minister, Fellowship of the Spiral Path, California

I pray to the birds.

I pray to the birds because I believe they will carry the messages of my heart upward. I pray to them because I believe in their existence, the way their songs begin and end each day— the invocations and the benedictions of Earth. I pray to the birds because they remind me of what I love rather than what I fear. And at the end of my prayers, they teach me how to listen.

Terry Tempest Williams
Environmentalist and author, Utah

God, in Your form of Beauty be with us.

May our hearts be broken. May our prayers be sufficient to feel the heartbreak of God.

God is not steel or any of the indestructible alloys we have created. God is a block of granite that stretches up from deep in the earth to the sky. God is the same stone etched by two white rivulets we call Current and Waterfall, flowing endlessly, carving the right and left hands whose names are also Beauty and Sorrow so that every drop rives the four chambers of the great heart. This is eternal. The Rising and the Falling. The Salt and the Sweet. The Burn and the Poultice. The Division and the Communion.

It never ceases: Dismay and Hope, Agony and Forgiveness. These are the four directions that Sun and Moon mark for us and that Day and Night illuminate. This is what we call East, West, North, South, thinking we can walk one way or another and not succumb to Windstorm, Earthquake, Volcano, or Drowning.

We want to be God in all the ways that are not the ways of God, in what we hope is indestructible or unmoving. But God is the most fragile, a bare smear of pollen, that scatter of yellow dust from the tree that tumbled over in a storm of grief and planted itself again. God is the death agony of the frog that cannot find water in the time of the drought of our creation. God is the scream of the rabbit caught in the fires we set. God is the One whose eyes never close and who hears everything.

Even if nothing can be fixed, let the vision reconstitute us through a pinhole in time and space—a vision of the lonely

God carrying the burden of universal sorrow. Let us take Her in our arms. Let us stroke His temples.

These are our tasks. Let us learn the secret languages of light again. Also the letters of the dark. Learn the flight patterns of birds, the syllables of wolf howl and bird song, the moving pantomime of branch and leaf, valleys and peaks of whale calls, the long sentences of ants moving in unison, the combinations and recombinations of clouds, the codices of stars. Let us, thus, reconstitute the world, sign by sign and melody by melody.

Let us sing the world back into the very Heart of the Holy Name of God.

Deena Metzger
Poet, California

Part 7

PRAYERS *of*
SOLIDARITY
and JUSTICE

We have only begun to know
the power that is in us if we would join
our solitudes in the communion of struggle.

DENISE LEVERTOV

We get so caught up in our personal circles of concern—our family, friends, work, and individual interests—that the reality of those less fortunate than ourselves rarely catches our attention. We may watch—and be genuinely touched by—TV news clips of refugees, war victims, and the poor in this country and abroad; but when the screen cuts to a bright commercial message, our minds cannot integrate the two opposing realities. This deadening process contracts and separates our experience of life by class, race, age, gender, and ethnicity.

Solidarity calls us to reach out across these boundaries that separate us. Solidarity with those who are subjected to injustice is based on the remembrance that we are brothers and sisters, part of one family many of whose members we have not yet met. Jesus' words, paraphrased here, instruct us in this kinship: "Inasmuch as you have shown kindness to these the least of my brethren—the stranger, the hungry, the sick, the imprisoned—you have shown kindness unto me." Jesus identifies himself with the stranger and the oppressed, just as we are asked to identify ourselves with our neighbor in the call to "love thy neighbor as thyself." These are strong, unequivocal words—yet how rarely are they practiced!

Solidarity is not only an inner practice—"a remembrance to love"—it also calls us to outer action. The prayers and reflections in this part of the book offer us guidance on this path. As the years of the new millennium unfold, we will have countless opportunities to heed and follow their counsel. Many of the writers here have known firsthand the suffering and injustice caused by the domination of one group over another. They cry out for liberation and renewal; they cry out for justice and kindness. In the words of Wanda Coleman:

> end the reign of false prosperity
> in the name of progress
> end the reign of arrogance
> in the name of education
> end the reign of denigration
> in the name of justice
> let the song go forth on spacious skies

In Part 7 we find words that are fierce, even defiant, because those who speak them have witnessed the cruelties heaped upon their people or upon the undefended life of the natural world. This fierceness is protective and courageous. And it is fitting that it be called forth as the new century dawns, for it is a fierceness born of love, not hate, like the roar of the she-bear protecting her young.

The spiritual life often is conceived of as "other-worldly" —a way of life primarily concerned with matters transcendent from the human-earth condition. This notion speaks more of the need of authorities to exert control and maintain the social status quo than it speaks to the truth at the heart of our religious traditions. Every major religious tradition is rooted in an ethic of love, compassion, and service. We cannot attain personal enlightenment or perfection or salvation without also standing in solidarity with "these the least of my brethren." As the prophet Muhammad has said, "Do you love your Creator? Love your fellow beings first."

Let us not fear those who suffer or who are simply different from us. Let us step beyond our shields and judgments and come into their presence; listen to what they want; pray with them in solidarity for the freedom and liberation of all.

231

The time for healing of the wounds has come.
The time to build is upon us . . .
We pledge ourselves to liberate all our people
from the continuing bondage of poverty, deprivation,
suffering, gender and other discrimination . . .
There is no easy road to freedom . . .
None of us acting alone can achieve success.
We must therefore act together as a united people,
for reconciliation, for nation building,
for the birth of a new world.

Nelson Mandela
President, Union of South Africa

Let us be present, each from her or his culture, each from her or his experience, and assume our responsibility for all life. Let us come together, in witness of difference, and embrace one another.

Let us see the child whose parents cannot be there, and put our arms around that child. Let us stand beside the woman abused by power, and recognize that all abuse of power diminishes our own humanity. Let us call upon the man who still believes he has a right to violate the lives of others, and let him know we will no longer tolerate his cowardice.

Let us join the growing chorus of those who will no longer be governed by those who cannot govern their own lives. Let us sound a mighty NO, echoing from mountaintops and ocean floors, through canyons and across deserts, jungles, forests, and farmlands, until that NO becomes a powerful YES. Let us hold life—from legions of humans to the tiniest flower—and recommit ourselves to nurturing its presence in all our lives.

Throughout past millennia, we have many times over reinvented nations, communities, and ourselves. We have walked toward progress and away from it. Today we have a single urgent choice: to dig our communal grave or to survive.

On the threshold of this new millennium, let us turn our backs on prejudice and greed, and—quietly, passionately—assume the only stance that offers hope to our great-great-grandchildren: for life, for the life in death, for peace with justice for all humankind.

Margaret Randall
Author and human rights activist, New Mexico

Prayers of Solidarity and Justice

234

Please pacify the uninterrupted miseries
and unbearable fears,
such as famines and sicknesses,
that torment powerless beings
completely oppressed by inexhaustible
and violent evils,
and henceforth lead us from suffering states
and place us in an ocean of happiness and joy.

Those who, maddened by the demons of delusion,
commit violent negative actions
that destroy both themselves and others
should be the object of our compassion.
May the hosts of undisciplined beings
fully gain the eye that knows
what to abandon and practice,
and be granted a wealth
of loving-kindness and friendliness.

Through the force of dependent-arising,
which by nature is profound
and empty of appearances,
the force of the Words of Truth,
the power of the kindness of the Three Jewels
and the true power of nondeceptive actions
and their effects;
may my prayer of truth
be accomplished quickly and without hindrance.

His Holiness the Fourteenth Dalai Lama
India

Prayers of Solidarity and Justice

For as long as space endures
And for as long as living beings remain,
Until then may I too abide
To dispel the misery of the world.

His Holiness the Dalai Lama asked that this, his favorite prayer, also be included.

*   *   *

In many parts of the world the people are searching for a solution that would link the two basic values: peace and justice. The two are like bread and salt for mankind. Every nation and every community has the inalienable right to these values; no conflicts can be resolved without doing everything possible to follow their road. Our difficult contemporary times require that these aspirations, which exist the world over, must be recognized.

Inscribed on the monument erected at the entrance to the Gdansk Shipyard in memory of those who died in December 1970 are the words of Psalm 29:11: "The Lord will give power to His people, the Lord will give His people the blessing of peace."

Let these words be our message of brotherhood and hope.

Lech Walesa
Former president of Poland and recipient,
Nobel Peace Prize, Poland

In those days, the Christ of Corcovado, overlooking the city of San Sebastin de Rio de Janeiro, shivered and came to life. Once cement and rock, He became flesh and blood. He extended his arms, reaching for the city and the world, opened his mouth, and said:

I feel pity for you, millions and millions of sisters and brothers, my little ones, driven off your land, solitary, hidden in jungles, piled up on the borders, fallen along so many paths, with no Samaritan to save you.

Blessed be you all, the poor, hungry, ailing, and the hopeless. My Father, giver of life, holds you in His Heart. He will inaugurate His Kingdom of Life, of justice, of tenderness, and of freedom, and you will be its first inhabitants.

Your blasphemies are not blasphemies for me. They are tormented supplications. For me, your individualism is not egoism. It is an iron will to survive.

Your painful passion has more stations than mine. You have enacted my redemptive Passion throughout the centuries.

Woe be to you, owners of power, who have for more than five hundred years sucked the blood of the workers. You have reduced them to cheap fuel for your machines to turn out unjust wealth. My Holy Name is even used to legitimize your order, which is disorder, and brings no progress to the people.

There is only one path of salvation for you, just one: join in solidarity with the struggles of the oppressed who search for bread, freedom, tenderness, and beauty, not only for themselves. Take on the project of the poor, which will be transformative for you, and there may be more life and freedom for all.

Blessed and blessed again be my black brothers and sisters, unjustly enslaved. The historic humiliation that you suffered has placed you in the heart of the celestial Father. You are the suffering Servant present in history, liberated through suffering, redeemed through blood, saved by the cross. You yourselves don't yet know the immense good that you bring to all, resisting, not losing the faith, singing, dancing, dreaming of the Promised Land. Until the final day, you have the right to cry out for rights, for recognition, for freedom, for a full life.

Blessed are those who struggle for the land in the countryside, working to prepare the earthen table for all the world's hungry people. Blessed are those who struggle for land in the city so that the sons and daughters of God may dwell there with dignity.

Blessed are the women who resist subjugation, who struggle for a new society in which men and women live together with differences, reciprocity, complementarity, and solidarity, for you will inaugurate a fraternal alliance.

Blessed are the millions of deprived and abandoned street children, victims of a society of exclusion. My Father will dry your tears, hold you tight, and play with you eternally because His son Jesus, while a child, was threatened with death and had to flee to Egypt.

Happy are the pastors, bishops, priests, brothers and sisters, and community organizers who humbly work to serve the people. Joyful are the movements that seek liberation for all, starting with the oppressed and marginalized. You take on the same cause I lived for, suffered for, and was crucified for. None of you are slandered for not belonging to my group or not speaking of me. You are also my disciples, and you are not far from my Kingdom.

238

Blessed are those who search for new paths to survival, new means of production, communal distribution, and shared consumption. I assure you that I will walk with you and we will find new forms of sharing.

Blessed are those who tearfully await the great aurora of liberation, fruit of divine grace and human struggle; for your eyes will see the glory of the sun's rays of justice. Blessed are those who preserve good will, feed the internal flame, and ever dream of a new world.

After saying these words of admonition, comfort, and promise, Christ turned back to stone, with arms extended and heart exposed. All should know that they are within his embrace, because they are eternally loved. And so it was then, now, and will be tomorrow in the sun and rain, in the wind and at night, for centuries and centuries, Amen.

Leonardo Boff
A leader of the Liberation Theology Movement, Brazil

Wakan Tanka, Creator, Great Spirit, look upon us and have pity. My heart cries out as I send my offerings. Grandfather, every day my *oyate*, the people, are stumbling or falling. The wind is very cold, and I have tears in my eyes as I turn toward the four winds. It is now dawn, grandfather. I hear you as I lift up my hand. I hear an eagle cry in the wind. Mitakuye, the Eagle, I pray to you—you who see the father, the sun. Bless our medicine and *unci make*, mother earth. Earth Mother I feel you with my bare feet, spirit in all things, Creator of all things. I feel the spirit of our ancestors who prayed on this red day June 21st.

239

I pray to you because I feel as if we are at the crossroads. I do not want to see my people suffer any more. I know the visions and dreams of our people are coming true. We are in a time of changes, and the sacred white buffalo calves are being born. I know the prophecies and visions of great leaders are coming true.

As I pray to the west grandfather *wakinyan oyate*, Thunder people, I pray with my *chanopa*, sacred pipe, and my offering in a humble way that peace and harmony be restored and sacred places be respected. Bring your blessing upon us as children of Earth Mother for health and happiness, Wakan Tanka. I feel better now as I send my voice to you, as I stand here in our circle of life where there is no ending and no beginning. I pray the sacred hoop of the nation and many nations upon Mother Earth, would mend and heal in peace; *Wolakota sunka wakan wicasa miyelo*. My name is Horseman.

Chief Arvol Looking Horse
Nineteenth-generation keeper of the Sacred White Buffalo Calf
Pipe, Lakota/Dakota and Nakota Nations, South Dakota

Let us pray for world peace, social justice, and environmental balance, which begins with our own breathing.

I breathe in calmly and breathe out mindfully.

Once I have seeds of peace and happiness within me, I try to reduce my selfish desire and reconstitute my consciousness. With less attachment to myself, I try to understand the structural violence in the world.

Linking my heart with my head, I perceive the world holistically, a sphere full of living beings who are all related to me.

I try to expand my understanding with love to help build a more nonviolent world.

I vow to live simply and offer myself to the oppressed.

By the grace of the Compassionate Ones and with the help of good friends, may I be a partner in lessening the suffering of the world so that it may be a proper habitat for all sentient beings to live in harmony during the next millennium.

Sulak Sivaraksa
Social activist and recipient of the Right Livelihood Award,
Santi Pracha Dhamma Institute, Thailand

Heavenly Mother, heavenly Father,
Holy and blessed is your true name.
We pray for your reign of peace to come,
We pray that your good will be done,
Let heaven and earth become one.
Give us this day the bread we need,
Give it to those who have none.
Let forgiveness flow like a river through us,
From each one to each one to each one.
Lead us to holy innocence
Beyond the evil of our days,
Come swiftly Mother, Father, come!
For yours is the power and the glory and the mercy—
Forever your name is All in One.

241

Parker Palmer
Quaker writer and teacher, Wisconsin

242

Ten thousand years I have been sleeping
and now I am being wakened.
My heavy eyelashes are the woods;
They are beckoning.
My heart, the clouds are surprised
because they are calling me, calling me.
My earth body is bedecked
with a thousand flowers,
Many breasts of mine,
the mountains joyfully rearing their tips,
They are calling! They are calling!
I want to embrace all the sad and the lost.
All wrongs my hands shall doom to death.
I am the defender of every woman
As I am the defender of my holy self.
Earthmother I am, the Only One;
Everything sprang from me;
I carry the seed of all creation;
I am the bestower of life alone.
Oh, oh, oh, I am awake!
Oh, I am answering the call . . .

Masika Szilagyi
Poet

Would you harbor me?
Would I harbor you?
Would you harbor me?
Would I harbor you?

Would you harbor a Christian?
   a Muslim?
   a Jew?
   a heretic?
   a convict?
   or a spy?
Would you harbor a runaway
      woman?
   or child?
   a poet?
   a prophet?
   a king?

Would you harbor an exile? or
   a refugee?
   a person living with AIDS?
Would you harbor a Tubman?
   a Garrett?
   a Truth?
   a fugitive? or
   a slave?
Would you harbor a Haitian?
   Korean? or
   Czech?
   a lesbian? or
   a gay?

Would you harbor me?
Would I harbor you?
Would you harbor me?
Would I harbor you?

243

Ysaye M. Barnwell
Singer and composer, Sweet Honey in the Rock,
Washington, D.C.

I listen to the women of Rio
when they try to speak
of street children murdered,
and my heart is breaking.

I listen to the women of Chernobyl
tell of childish blank faces
grown old and lifeless,
and my heart is breaking.

I listen to the women of Bhopal
whisper the grotesqueness
of deformity and disease,
and my heart is breaking.

I listen to the women of Addis Ababa
describing empty stomachs
and drought,
and my heart is breaking.

I listen to the women of Cyprus
and Ireland and Sri Lanka
and South Africa.
I hear conflict's pain,
and my heart is breaking.

But also,
I listen to the Madres, and the Women in Black
and the African mamas. I listen to
the young women of Asia and the Pacific Rim.
I listen to the female voices of North Africa
and the Middle East and Eastern Europe.
And I hear

Prayers of Solidarity and Justice

the Power of Everywoman,
Everywhere.
Then, I rejoice,
I hope,
I take heart.

Elayne Clift
Poet, Vermont

*   *   *

For Christians all around the world, the year 2000 will be a time to remember with thanksgiving the One whose birthday it commemorates. But along with that thanksgiving will, I hope, come some thoughtful reflection on mistakes we have made in the past and a determination to reflect our Founder's teachings still better in the future.

Our faith has, at its best, never confined itself to a concern for any one section of society. We find our true selves in the service of others of whatever nation, race, social status, or creed. My hope and vision is that the Church would learn afresh what Jesus himself taught us: that "the greatest among us must be the servant of all."

Most Rev. George L. Carey
Archbishop of Canterbury, England

The universe unfolds through a continuous process of breakdown, chaos, and spontaneous eruptions into new levels of order and meaning. This process occurs in every manifestation of life: the stars, the planets, earth, the continents, the oceans, plants, animals, humans.

In our human world, the old forms are breaking down and chaos threatens to annihilate everything. But, like the universe, we too will erupt into new levels of order and meaning. Consciousness is our unique reflection of the universe: we are the universe in a conscious mode. We participate most intimately in the great unfolding. We journey together.

Leader:	Response:
In the face of growing darkness	*We journey together*
In the face of ecological decline	*We journey together*
In the face of social upheaval	*We journey together*
In the face of growing uncertainty	*We journey together*

All: *In the face of growing darkness, we journey together toward the light.*

Leader:	Response:
As we search for glimpses of truth	*We journey together*
As we search for signs of possibility	*We journey together*
As we search for heralds of a new era	*We journey together*
As we search for angels of hope	*We journey together*

Prayers of Solidarity and Justice

All: *As we search for glimpses of truth, we journey together toward new levels of meaning.*

Leader:	Response:
As we build our world out of chaos	*We journey together*
As we build our world out of shattered illusions of superiority	*We journey together*
As we build our world out of our inadequate institutions	*We journey together*
As we build our world out of our unfair sharing of resources	*We journey together*

All: *As we build our world out of the chaos, we journey together toward a new era of justice.*

Leader:	Response:
As the universe unfolds	*We journey together*
As the universe unfolds through spontaneous communion	*We journey together*
As the universe unfolds through new levels of meaning	*We journey together*
As the universe unfolds through new forms of life	*We journey together*

All: *As the universe unfolds, we journey together in God's great becoming.*

Rev. Daniel Martin
International Communities for the
Renewal of the Earth (ICRE), New York

248

We put our arms around each other
a pair of ordinary tax-paying human arms
not to rest them
but to harden them
a pair of ordinary concrete-accustomed
and marketed human arms
a pair of ordinarily needing
a pair of ordinarily hugging
human arms
we put them around each other
they are health-insured and ordinarily dressed
a pair of ordinary love-interpreting
human arms
how strong they are
sovereign, independent—
no matter where
no matter what the hour
no matter what the season
suddenly and for all time
human arms
without speculation
we put them around each other
as if to show that their powerlessness
doesn't exist

Marianne Larsen
Poet, Denmark

We are female human beings poised at the time of the new millennium. We are the majority of our species, yet we have dwelt in the shadows. We are the invisible, the illiterate, the laborers, the refugees, the poor.

And we vow: No more.

We are the women who hunger—for rice, home, freedom, each other, ourselves.

We are the women who thirst—for clean water and laughter, literacy and love. We have existed at all times, in every society. We have survived femicide. We have rebelled—and left clues.

We are continuity, weaving future from past, logic with lyric.

We are the women who stand in our senses and shout YES.

We are the women who wear broken bones, voices, minds, hearts—but we are the women who dare to whisper NO.

We are the women whose souls no fundamentalist cage can contain.

We are the women who refuse to permit the sowing of death in our gardens, air, rivers, seas.

We are the women men warned us about.

We are each precious, unique, necessary. We are strengthened and blessed and relieved at not having to be all the same. We are the daughters of longing. We are the mothers in labor to birth the politics of the twenty-first century.

Robin Morgan, 1994 Women's Environment and
Development Organization Global Strategies Meeting

Prayers of Solidarity and Justice

Dear God
Your will is that we may be one.
We thank you that you call us into communion
with you and with each other.
Your generosity and mercy are always
taking us by surprise.
We bless you for the vision of
inclusion, solidarity, and compassion
which breaks us open, widens our sympathies,
and enlarges our hearts.

We commend into your gracious care
all those whom it would be easy for us to forget—
the homeless and the hungry,
the addicted and the lost,
abandoned souls and hurting children.

We thank you for the imagination and generosity
of those who minister
in the name of love and compassion
to those who are most in need.

Let us, together,
seek to serve the needy, the rejected, and the forgotten.

Confront our indifference,
challenge our boundaries, surprise us with joy.

Dear Christ,
look upon us in this suffering and glorious world,
and keep our sympathy

Prayers of Solidarity and Justice

and pity fresh
and our faces heavenward
lest we grow hard.

Amen.

Rev. Alan Jones
Dean of Grace Cathedral, San Francisco, California

*   *   *

And now, I am supposed to say to you, "Go in peace." But how can I say, "Go in peace," with you going out into a world where you are insecure, whether at home or on your neighborhood street?

Out into a world where race is set against race and ethnic cleansing is a name for genocide?

Out into a world where people are hungry and homeless, while their governments squander billions of dollars on instruments of destruction that they dare not use?

Out into a world where every night millions of mothers watch their children sink into a hungry slumber, only to awaken (if they awaken) to another hungry tomorrow?

With a world like that out there, how can I say to you, "Go in peace"?

But I dare say, "Go in peace," because Jesus says, "I give you my peace"; but remember, he who says, "I give you my peace" also says, "If you would be my disciple and [thereby] have my peace, take up your cross and follow me!" So I dare say, "Go in peace"—if you dare!

Clinton M. Marsh
Presbyterian Peace Fellowship, Georgia

Prayers of Solidarity and Justice

Lord, when did we see you hungry?

I was hungry and you were flying around the moon.
I was hungry and you told me to wait.
I was hungry and you formed a committee.
I was hungry and you talked about other things.

I was hungry and you told me:
"There is no reason."
I was hungry
and you had bills to pay for weapons.
I was hungry and you told me:
"Now machines do that kind of work."
I was hungry and you said:
"Law and order come first."
I was hungry and you said:
"There are always poor people."
I was hungry and you said:
"My ancestors were hungry too."
I was hungry and you said:
"After age fifty, no one will hire you."
I was hungry and you said:
"God helps those in need."
I was hungry and you said:
"Sorry, stop by again tomorrow."

Anonymous twentieth-century Lutheran prayer, France
Translated by Mary-Theresa McCarthy

I've never been good at praying in the conventional sense. I'm more likely to pray in the strangest places.

Flying is one of my least favorite things to do. Yet the darkened cabin of a 747 as it hurtles through the night sky some 37,000 feet above Mother Earth has—many times—been my church.

More than a few of the journeys I undertake are on behalf of the children of the world. Witnessing cruelties perpetrated on our children disturbs me deeply, and my Irish temper becomes hard to control. It is only through prayer that I can turn that anger around and begin to do constructive rather than destructive things to help alleviate at least a little of children's suffering.

My car also serves as my church. Driving alone I ask God to guide me—both on the road and in my work.

I pray for a world where children will be treated with love and dignity. But praying, alone, is not sufficient. Just as tears without action are wasted sentiment, prayer without action is futile. After all, God did not create the mess this world is in; we did!

Yes, by all means, pray. But have the courage to help God change the terrible wrongs of our world.

As my beloved friend, Monsignor Michael Buckley, said many times at the conclusion of Mass: "May the peace of Christ thoroughly disturb you."

Betty Williams
1976 Nobel Peace Laureate, Founder of
World Centers of Compassion for Children, Florida

We continue to follow the spirit of the people who have gone before us, who have handed down to us laws for the land and the right way to establish human relationships for the maintenance of our religion and culture.

Despite what people from mining companies and others might like to think, our country still makes sense to us, its meaning communicated through sacred sites which crisscross the continent. We continue to love our land, the country that gives us life, gives us our social, political, and family institutions.

We will not continue to sit at the foot of your table and watch you grow fat off our land.

We will not continue to accept the scraps that you choose to throw down to us and then threaten to take away.

We will not give up our struggle for recognition, independence, and dignity.

Like our forebears, we will not die, we will not go away; our particular cultural genius has roots that reach back into time, beyond your recorded history, and continue to sustain us.

Pat Dodson
Australian Aborigine

This prayer is addressed to my fellow creatures.

O great, powerful, and ever-swarming tribe, I pray, with the most sincere passion, that you will be as conscious of your potential for evil as for good. Some of us have always been willing to resort even to murder, and all of us, it is reasonable to fear, are potential offenders. But fortunately, our violent angers, our greed, selfishness, sexual aggressiveness, and pride are counterbalanced by our ability to love, to smile, to feed, to clothe, to teach, and in other ways to attend to the needs of others.

Some moral lessons are muddled, but others are clear: that we would rather be touched affectionately than struck painfully, to be fed than be denied sustenance, to be free rather than in chains, to be loved rather than despised. Consequently, we should seize every opportunity to treat others in precisely the way we wish to be treated, to avoid committing acts we criticize in others.

I pray that we will.

Steve Allen
Musician, songwriter, comedian, and author, California

If I were to spit upon the revered black stone in Mecca during the height of the annual pilgrimage, I would be slain on the spot by enraged pilgrims for daring to profane the sacred symbol of Islam. An Israeli soldier's bullet in the back would be my deserved fate for scrawling graffiti upon the Wailing Wall in Jerusalem. Nor would I be long for this world if I were to defecate upon the floor of the Golden Temple of the Sikhs. Life would not be pleasant for me if I took a hammer to the *Pietà* in the Vatican, for we humans hold our creations dear, and we deal harshly with those who fail to share our reverence for old stone walls, meteorites, marble statues, icons, and architecture.

What we love, we protect. What we revere, we defend. What we value, we will die for—and of course not hesitate to kill for. Yet each and every day, humans enter the most sacred and reverential cathedrals of the natural world—the redwood forests of Northern California or the rain forests of Amazonia—and each and every day we profanely rape these great mysteries with chainsaws and bulldozers.

Where is the rage over the destruction of the rain forests? Where is the violent anger at those who foul the oceans? Where is the sorrow for the hundreds of species that humankind has condemned to the oblivion of extinction?

The natural world is an abstraction to a species that has too much heaven on its mind. We worship a creator molded in the image of Man and desecrate nature out of jealous anger for its independence from man.

We do not see whales; we see oil. We do not see trees; we see toilet paper or houses. We do not see rivers; we see hydro power. We do not see an ocean; we see a sewer.

Prayers of Solidarity and Justice

Gone forever is the dodo, the passenger pigeon, the auk, and the Caroline parakeet. Never again will our planet be graced by the buffalo wolf, the Atlas bear, the Barbary lion, or the Steller's sea cow. No more shall grow the moth orchid, the wine palm, or the exotic hau kuahiwi. The realms of the insects, the mollusks, the amphibians, and the reptiles have fared no better—all the victims of the arrogant ignorance of man.

Our brief and brutal reign has spanned such a minute period within the age of the Earth, yet our destructions have expunged species and habitats that graced the Earth for millions of years prior to our existence. We are generating the sixth extinction at a rate one thousand times greater than the previous five, the last being sixty-five million years ago.

We give it little thought, wiping out the very memory of extinct species as a mopping up maneuver to appease our conscience.

Into the future we dream of great conquests of planets. We create traveling public relations teams to present ourselves to ourselves as a moral and righteous species. In the name of our anthropocentric philosophies we can destroy anything and everything and call it progress.

The question is, How long can we continue this insanity of living in defiance of the laws of ecology?

If we ignore the law of biodiversity, our ecosystems will collapse further with the loss of each nonreplaced species. If we ignore the law of interdependence, we will find ourselves alone and abandoned, the final victims of our own arrogance. If we ignore the law of finite growth, we will find ourselves choking on our own filth as the value of human life diminishes in proportion to the increasing multitudes of our own spawn.

Maybe it is appropriate that man is a primate. When all has been said and done, at least our condemnation can be tempered by the simple biological fact that we are monkeys.

And like good little monkeys, we saw no evil, heard no evil, and spoke no evil as we basked in the glory of the fading empire of anthropocentrism, insulated from the pain of the myriad of vanquished and vanishing species, forgetting that we are a part of that which we mindlessly destroy, and as such, we will be our own last victims.

Captain Paul Watson
Co-founder, Greenpeace, and founder,
Sea Shepherd Conservation Society, California

Let us pray, brothers
for those who have filled their pockets
with stones
and whose fists are still clenched
for those who because they have not loved
have not been loved
and bury their rocky selves
across from the coast of affection.

Let us pray for those who ruin innocence
with reckless velocity.
Let us pray
for those who get stuck
in bitterness
and throw punches that bruise.

Let us pray
for those who will not be happy
and will not become what they had hoped to be.
Let us pray
for him who flees from himself
and loses himself in the sordid world
where residue gravitates
and is hurled into the fright of the streets.

Let us pray
that we may live in one nation
"with all and for the well-being of all"
without mutually devaluing ourselves.
Let us pray, brothers
for an infinite universal embrace.

Rafael Bordao
"Prayer for a New World," Cuban poet, New York

Prayers of Solidarity and Justice

We evoke your name, Avalokiteshvara. We aspire to learn your way of listening in order to help relieve the suffering in the world. You know how to listen in order to understand. We evoke your name in order to practice listening with all our attention and open-heartedness. We will sit and listen without any prejudice. We will sit and listen without judging or reacting. We will sit and listen in order to understand. We will sit and listen so attentively that we will be able to hear what the other person is saying and also what has been left unsaid. We know that just by listening deeply we already alleviate a great deal of pain and suffering in the other person.

We evoke your name, Manjushri. We aspire to learn your way, which is to be still and to look deeply into the heart of things and into the hearts of people. We will look with all our attention and open-heartedness. We will look with unprejudiced eyes. We will look without judging or reacting We will look deeply so that we will be able to see and understand the roots of ill-being, the impermanent and selfless nature of all that is. We will practice your way of using the sword of understanding to cut through the bonds of ill-being, thus freeing ourselves and other species.

We evoke your name, Samantabhadra. We aspire to practice your aspiration to act with the eyes and heart of compassion. We vow to bring joy to one person in the morning and to ease the pain of one person in the afternoon. We know that the happiness of others is our own happiness, and we vow to practice joy on the path of service. We know that every word, every look, every action, and every smile can bring happiness to others. We know that if we practice wholeheartedly, we ourselves may become an inexhaustible source of peace and joy for our loved ones and for all species.

Prayers of Solidarity and Justice

We evoke your name, Ksitigarbha. We aspire to learn your way so as to be present where there is darkness, suffering, oppression, and despair, so that we may bring light, hope, relief, and liberation to those places. We are determined not to forget about or abandon those who are in desperate situations. We shall do our best to establish contact with them when they cannot find a way out of their suffering and when their cries for help, justice, equality, and human rights are not heard. We know that hell can be found in many places on earth, and we do not want to contribute to making more hells on earth. Rather, we want to help unmake the hells which already exists. We shall practice to realize the qualities of perseverance and stability which belong to the earth, so that like the earth we can always be supportive and faithful to those who need us.

261

Plum Village Community
Founded by Thich Nhat Hanh,
Vietnamese Zen Buddhist, France

O deep waters breaking. good. wash away

end this soullessness where
weakness is fostered, fed on, yet the weak punished
disproportionately for their weaknesses
where harmless indiscretions are fodder
for the lies of bigots, fascists, and misanthropes
where community is counterfeit
end the reign of the bogus in the name of the correct
let the just go forth

262

o deep waters rising. mother the good. wash away

end this soullessness where
the hypocrites & heartless in power force an
inhumane asceticism on the powerless
litigate their advocates into ineffectiveness
starve the heartful into meanness. where the worker
is devalued and the different valueless
end the reign of fakery in the name of the pious
let the brave find their fists

o deep waters roiling. father the good. wash away

end this soullessness where
wounded lives fester unhealed and unexpressed
where quality and tenderness are beyond
the means of the needy, where the dysfunctional
are consigned to prisons streets state crematoriums
where cartoon cults console the disarranged
(ever the ravenous devour the earth)
end the reign of callousness in the name of economy
let the lovers go forth

Prayers of Solidarity and Justice

o deep waters rising. manchild the good. wash away

end this soullessness where
entertainment is religion, trickery
and cruelty are legitimized, institutions are
founded on fear, tradition is the calcification
of denial, sincerity a character flaw
where affectation rules over authenticity
end the reign of murderers in the guise of law and order
let the long-silenced speak

o deep waters rising. womanchild the good. wash away

end this soullessness where
the deceitful and the greed-mongers flourish
thugs control the flow of beauty and the artless
control the artful. where abuse for profit
is rewarded where self-censorship is rewarded where
cowardice is rewarded and dark brilliance shunned

o deep water risings. gatherings of the good for the good

end the reign of false prosperity
in the name of progress
end the reign of arrogance
in the name of education
end the reign of denigration
in the name of justice
let the song go forth on spacious skies

o deep water rushings wash good at dawn's gloryrise

Wanda Coleman
Poet, California

Listen
with the night falling we are saying thank you
we are stopping on the bridges to bow from the railings
we are running out of the glass rooms
with our mouths full of food to look at the sky
and say thank you
we are standing by the water looking out
in different directions.

back from a series of hospitals back from a mugging
after funerals we are saying thank you
after the news of the dead
whether or not we knew them we are saying thank you
looking up from tables we are saying thank you
in a culture up to its chin in shame
living in the stench it has chosen we are saying thank you

over telephones we are saying thank you
in doorways and in the backs of cars and in elevators
remembering wars and the police at the back door
and the beatings on stairs we are saying thank you
in the banks that use us we are saying thank you
with the crooks in office with the rich and fashionable
unchanged we go on saying thank you thank you

with the animals dying around us
our lost feelings we are saying thank you
with the forests falling faster than the minutes
of our lives we are saying thank you
with the words going out like cells of a brain
with the cities growing over us like the earth
we are saying thank you faster and faster

with nobody listening we are saying thank you
we are saying thank you and waving
dark though it is

W. S. Merwin
Poet, Hawaii

*   *   *

And then all that has divided us will merge
And then compassion will be wedded to power
And then softness will come to a world
    that is harsh and unkind
And then both men and women will be gentle
And then both women and men will be strong
And then no person
    will be subject to another's will
And then all will be rich and free and varied
And then the greed of some
    will give way to the needs of many
And then all will share equally
    in the earth's abundance
And then all will care
    for the sick and the weak and the old
And then all will cherish life's creatures
And then all will live
    in harmony with each other and the earth.
And then everywhere
    will be called Eden once again.

Judy Chicago
Artist and author

Prayers of Solidarity and Justice

Part 8

REFLECTIONS
on POLITICS,
ECONOMICS,
and MORALITY

In that tiny space between all the givens is freedom.
SUE BENDER

How shall we govern ourselves, loyal to our commitments to justice and liberty? And what shall we count as work worthy of our dreams? These two questions are at the heart of the following reflections on politics and economics. What makes good policy, and what makes good work?

The writers in Part 8 reflect in diverse ways on the values they wish to see as foundations for our political and economic structures. The need for foundational values is stressed by the Burmese leader Aung San Suu Kyi, whose nonviolent resistance to the Burmese military regime has won the world's respect:

> The challenge we now face is for the different nations and peoples of the world to agree on a basic set of human values, which will serve as a unifying force in the development of a genuine global community.

The emphasis in this section on articulating basic political and economic values goes hand in hand with personal action. We need to do more than remind ourselves of our good intentions, these authors say. We need to *act* in the service of our values. "Let us move," writes Riane Eisler, "from compassion for the world's poor to changing our global economic system." This call to action is all the more poignant—and necessary—

as we acknowledge the immensity and anonymity of our political and economic institutions and their commitment to preserving an unjust status quo.

As we enter the third millennium, according to a United Nations report, the richest fifth of the world's people accounts for 86 percent of private consumption, while the poorest fifth consumes only 1.3 percent of the pie. And this gap continues to widen. In the industrialized countries alone there are over 100 million people who are homeless. The wealth of the richest 225 people in the world equals the annual income of nearly half of humanity. These statistics arise in the context of global environmental decline, widespread destruction of animal and plant habitat, massive pollution, and depletion of finite resources.

The astounding political and economic lie of the possibility—and desirability—of ever-continuing economic "growth" based on depleting the earth and diminishing the liberty of others reminds us of the growth of a tumor, destroying the body it feeds upon. Self-interest and greed fuel this lie. Their very nature cannot abide the necessity or beauty of limits. Yet all life thrives or dies within the limits of ecosystems; each niche a species expands into is, by its very nature, circumscribed. Our species, even though we are named "sapiens"—the wise—has been voraciously consuming the ecological capital on which our survival depends.

This is why people of conscience and communities of faith must speak out at this time. Traditions of resistance—for example, the Quaker commitment to "speak truth to power," the Jewish tradition of the prophets who challenged the kings, the lineage of "engaged Buddhism," and the Christian response of not capitulating to Caesar—are critically important for our world. If enough people step out of the lie into the truth, we have the chance to reverse the damage of past centuries, bind up the wounds of our people, and turn from excessive consumption and concentrations of power to communities of justice and generations of peace.

How do we move out of the lie and into the truth? Rabbi Michael Lerner offers us the first step:

> Let us reject cynicism about the possibility of building a very different kind of world—a world in which ethical and spiritual behavior become the norm. Let us agree that in the coming years we will insist on a "new bottom line" of love and solidarity and spiritual sensitivity. . . .

We must take this responsibility, each in our own way. Whether or not we achieve success in our lifetimes should not affect our motivation to act. Each of us must speak our truth to power and work for a freer and more equitable world, if for no other reason than to sustain qualities in our own hearts and spirits that would be destroyed by inaction and apathy.

Faith is not enough. We must act on our faith. Inner healing is not enough. We must heal our world. Spiritual practice is not enough. We must have the spiritual courage to stand up against injustice.

Let us move from charity to the world's hungry to changing the conditions that create hunger, from horror at the international sex trade of little girls to action to stop it, from compassion for the world's poor to changing our global economic system.

Together let us create a world where love is manifested through a politics and economics of caring, where caretaking is the most honored and rewarded work, where all children are safe from violence in their families and in their communities. Let us liberate our Mother Earth from those who would conquer and despoil nature. Let us remember that we all share the DNA of one Eve who lived in Africa millions of years ago. Let us treat one another as who we are: sisters and brothers in the miracle and mystery we call life.

Riane Eisler
Author, president, The Center for
Partnership Studies, California

Reflections on Politics, Economics, and Morality

The true development of human beings involves much more than mere economic growth. At its heart there must be a sense of empowerment and inner fulfillment. This alone will ensure that human and cultural values remain paramount in a world where political leadership is often synonymous with tyranny and the rule of a narrow elite. People's participation in social and political transformation is the central issue of our time. This can be achieved only through the establishment of societies that place human worth above power, and liberation above control. In this paradigm, development requires democracy, the genuine empowerment of the people. The challenge we now face is for the different nations and peoples of the world to agree on a basic set of human values, which will serve as a unifying force in the development of a genuine global community.

273

Aung San Suu Kyi
Democratic leader and recipient, Nobel Peace Prize, Burma

I wish in the coming millennium for but one thing: democracy. Democracy of, by, and for the people. Participatory democracy, direct democracy, strong democracy. Because democracy empowers, and empowerment confers the means by which we can stop wishing and realize our own purposes—on our own. Because democracy is the condition under which liberty can be secured without offending justice. Because democracy is the means by which justice can be invoked without corrupting liberty.

The democracy for which I yearn is not a particular constitution or a singular kind of government: it is a way of living, a mode of being. A way of being together without surrendering freedom; a mode of preserving solitude without abjuring cooperation; a way of acknowledging conflict without inviting war.

Democracy is not about electing those who are to govern us; it is about governing ourselves. Democracy is not a destination but a journey; it is a process rather than an end. More than speaking well, it means knowing how to listen well. It means we speak among ourselves and not just to leaders or to followers. It depends on imagination: the capacity to see deep into others, down and beyond color, accent, nationality.

Democracy must be won—and then rewon; and still again possessed and repossessed, generation by generation. No one was ever gifted freedom; it must be taken.

I say democracy is the first principle of humankind because it is the principle by which our kind is made human.

I say it is our last best hope in the new millennium, as it has been in the millennium just past.

I say democracy. With Walt Whitman and Jean Jacques Rousseau, with Thomas Jefferson and Nelson Mandela, with Paul Robeson and Mohandas Gandhi and Susan B. Anthony, with Frederick Douglass and bloodied John Brown, I say democracy now.

Benjamin R. Barber
Director, The Walt Whitman Center for the Culture and Politics
of Democracy, Rutgers University, New Jersey

275

An enormous conflict between words and deeds is prevalent today: everyone talks about freedom, democracy, justice, human rights . . . about peace and saving the world from nuclear apocalypse; and at the same time, everyone, more or less, consciously or unconsciously, serves those values and ideals only to the extent necessary to serve himself and his "worldly" interests, personal interests, group interests, power interests, property interests, and state or great-power interests. . . . So the power structures apparently have no other choice than to sink deeper into this vicious maelstrom, and contemporary people apparently have no other choice than to wait around until the final inhibition drops away. . . . But who should begin? Who should break this vicious circle? . . . Responsibility cannot be preached but only borne, and the only possible place to begin is with oneself. . . .

Václav Havel
President, Czech Republic, Poet and playwright

Reflections on Politics, Economics, and Morality

If all goes well
The police
    out of total boredom
        will go home
Borders will disappear
Even the toy factories
will stop making arms

If all goes well
there will be no Premier
        President
Savior of Democracy
King
    Emperor
            Tyrant

If all goes well
they will stop
    trying to convince us
with lies.

If all goes well
Ayatollahs
        Great Lamas
                Popes
will allow God
to once more be human
                dolphin
                    extraterrestrial
cedar and seagull
    herb and star
sea

Reflections on Politics, Economics, and Morality

mountain

    insect

    dog

    and cat.

If all goes well
    if all goes well
as long as the nova's hour
    doesn't come
or the black hole
    doesn't absorb our dreams
we will take our children's hands
so they may feel
    protected and our gentleness.
We will share our games
We will surrender our kisses
I will laugh
    I will sing
I will complain of work's hassles
I'll count my gray hairs
and until the very end
    I will delight
in the adventure
of the sensation
    of emotion
        and thought.

If all goes well
    If all goes well

If all goes well.

Juan Antillon Montealegre, Poet, Costa Rica
Translated by Joseph Richey

Reflections on Politics, Economics, and Morality

278

From the most troubled century of the bloodiest millennium in humanity's four-million-year history has emerged a new awakening, a new search for our place in the evolutionary journey of life on earth. For two centuries, our civilization has striven to perfect the technology, economics, and culture of domination. May the coming centuries usher in a heightened awareness of our true embeddedness in the web of life. May we overturn patterns of domination and learn to embody cooperation and harmony in our towns and neighborhoods and in the world community.

In the closing decades of the twentieth century, we have learned to hear the voices of those who speak for the forests, rivers, and oceans. We listen to our neighbors, who are resisting toxic contamination and seeking environmental justice. We are learning the stories of the tree huggers of India, the indigenous defenders of the rain forests, and the Mayan rebels of southern Mexico, who offer both an urgent call of alarm and a resonating message of hope. It is a hope for a new revolution in our society, in our relationships with one another and with all of life: a revolution that is gentle but uncompromising, realistic but utopian, one that embraces our interdependence and celebrates our creativity. Let us raise our voices. Let us cry out to all the earth-loving people around the globe and become a united voice for healing cooperation and a peaceful, more compassionate future.

Brian Tokar
Author and educator, Institute for Social Ecology, Vermont

Just as serfdom, slavery, colonialism, and apartheid ended, so also will detrimental globalization, threats to biodiversity, indebtedness, and legalized corruption, giving way to governance that will be responsible and accountable to people and all other forms of life. Such evils violate the basic rights to life on our planet and will therefore be challenged and defeated by visionary leaders and peoples from all nations determined to give hope now and in the future.

Wangari Maathai
Leader of Women's Green Belt Movement, Kenya

*   *   *

Overconsumption by the world's fortunate is nearly as responsible for the Earth's crisis as are spiraling birth rates. One billion people live in luxury unprecedented in any previous era. Twenty percent of the people consume 80 percent of the Earth's resources. They are the world's consuming class, the car-driving, meat-eating, throwaway society. Support for the affluent lifestyle of the world's wealthiest has been the driving force for damage to the Earth's resource base. Because of overconsumption we have come to the brink of the global economy's limits, and our runaway appetite for consumption threatens to overwhelm even the best efforts to forestall environmental decline.

Susan J. Clark
Environmental activist, Washington State

A sustainable economy represents nothing less than a higher social order—one as concerned with future generations as with our own, and more focused on the health of the planet and the poor than on material acquisitions and military might. While it is a fundamentally new endeavor, with many uncertainties, it is far less risky than continuing with business as usual.

280

Sandra Postel and Christopher Flavin
Worldwatch Institute, Washington, D.C.

*　　*　　*

Open the storage units
Unlock every second home
Distribute every safebox jewel
Take down the fences so any may pass
Burn the titles of your past
Invite the wild to backyards
　　and mark the dead with trees
Throw away your watches,
　　take the time you need
Scatter the riches written in
　　the ledgers of far-away banks
Wash your eyes with water and
　　look again
Plant the seed of your dream,
　　your heart, your care.
May your backyard be a garden for you,
　　for me, for all beings.

Gigi Coyle
Co-director, Ojai Foundation, California

May the rivers of wealth
be undammed and flow
freely over the Earth.
May the gifts move through
increased hands until
all people experience the
abundance of life.

Marion Rockefeller Weber
The Flow Fund Circle, California

*　　*　　*

The twentieth century started late and ended early. When Global Capital englobed the world ten years ago the millennium was already born.

Every human relation reduced to greed and exchange, the human measured by money; the global media become our Imagination.

A prayer for the third millennium? By the Seven Eyes of Allah I pray for the downfall of Global Capital—for the destruction of the pseudo-Enlightenment rationalism of sameness and separation.

I pray for an insurrectionary and federated culture of difference and presence—for indigenous, regional, anti-hegemonic, molecular resistance—and for an urban Zapatismo.

History will not begin again on the Internet, but in the inspiration to imagine empirical freedoms. *Tierra y Libertad!*
Love Truth Peace Freedom & Justice

Peter Lamborn Wilson
Author, Moorish Orthodox Church of America, New York

Reflections on Politics, Economics, and Morality

Born in a century of war and injustice, the United Nations is humanity's best hope for a future of peace and justice.

For the first time in recorded history, the nations of the world are banded together for peace. The United Nations represents a hope of humanity for a world that is not only at peace but promises people a better life and a future with freedom and equality.

An effective United Nations can be achieved only if people everywhere support it. In the past century we have created the tools for instant global communication as well as the weapons for instant global destruction. We now have the means to enhance the dreams of humanity for a better world. An effective global community—as represented by the United Nations—can be the legacy of our generation.

We can now realize that freedom from fear and want and suffering for one nation is inseparably bound up with freedom from fear and want and suffering for all nations.

Today, as we enter a new millennium, may we understand more than ever before what it means to be our brothers' and sisters' keepers.

Irving Sarnoff
Friends of the United Nations, California

The public fascination with the sinking of the *Titanic* may be attributed to its power as a metaphor of our modern industrial world—the arrogance of wealth and power, the crass disregard of human life and the natural world, and the persistent denial that any disaster could happen to us.

Christians are not exempt from these sins. Such blindness, ignorance, and alienation—that Christian congregations should witness nature being desecrated through poisoning of the atmosphere, degradation of soil and water, deforestation and species extinction, yet hardly raise a voice of protest!

The environmental crisis is a spiritual crisis. Scientists and theologians alike are telling us that our stewardship of Earth, and the worldview on which it is based, must change if we are to reverse the deterioration we have inflicted on the planet. A spiritual revolution is urgently required. The Christian Church can contribute unique gifts—namely, the biblical story and rituals that reinforce human responsibility to care for Earth. As expressed in John 3:16, "God so loved the world. . . ." God's salvation is extended to the whole cosmos.

Jesus Christ, our savior, guide and mentor, tells us to repent, to love God and our neighbor. The church now must expand the concept of neighbor to include the whole creation. Just as we meet Christ in our human neighbor, we meet Christ in every part of creation. Understanding human history in the context of the spiritual and physical history of the universe is a first step toward repentance—a humble acceptance of a healing worldview.

Rev. Finley Schaef and Elizabeth Dyson
North American Coalition for
Christianity and Ecology, New York

The golden thread of spiritual realization that links together all the great religious traditions of the world needs to be strengthened, so that as we enter the new millennium we can shed the baggage of fanaticism, fundamentalism, and bigotry that so cruelly distorted the twentieth century, and move into a new dimension of an integrated human being living in a harmonious global society.

The Vedas, the most ancient living scriptures of the human race, teach that this entire cosmos is permeated by the divine power, and that each human being encapsulates a spark of divinity. Fanning that spark into the blazing fire of spiritual realization is one of the major goals of human existence. The other is to work for the welfare of all beings—human as well as nonhuman. We must raise the level of human consciousness to comprehend the tremendous creative potentialities of the human mind and spirit.

Karan Singh
Member of Parliament, India

The challenge of the new millennium is to reunite the secular with the sacred, the inner world of spirit with the outer world of service. With the very survival of people and the planet at risk, we hear the cry for a conscious integration of spirit into all aspects of our lives. The health of our civilization depends continually on the enlivened wholeness and spiritual freedom of its citizens. We cannot address the larger issues of our society without simultaneously freeing our own inner lives.

285

Perhaps, as we reflect back on this century, we will come to realize that it is not enough to want to do good. It is not enough to convince our nations to do good. We must learn a great deal more about the wisdom of doing good.

Let us enter this new age with the hope that, when we see clearly, we will discover what the great spiritual traditions have taught for centuries; simply that as we enhance our inner capacity for wholeness and freedom, we strengthen our outer capacity to love and serve.

Let us pray to live from our hearts. Let us pray that we enliven what the old Hasidic tradition defines as dawn—that when we look into the face of another human being and have enough light to see ourselves, then we have awakened, then we have opened the living moment of compassion where night ends and day begins.

Robert Lehman
The Fetzer Institute, Michigan

Let us admit it: our vain attempt to build a glorious civilization by ignoring, even denying, God, has failed miserably. The twentieth century—the most secular century ever—has also been the most violent century in human history. As the century draws to a close, rapid globalization is bringing to the fore some of the inequities and injustices that divide humankind. It is only too apparent that in politics and economics, as in culture and social relations, moral considerations have little weight or value.

This is why at the end of the millennium our greatest need is to remember God. The remembrance of God is not some fanatical plea for a return to rigid religious dogma. To remember God is to uphold justice; for justice, the Koran tells us, was the mission of each and every prophet. To remember God is to strive for peace; it is to uphold freedom; it is to ensure the equality of all human beings. The remembrance of God is the expression of compassion and kindness in our daily lives.

To remember God, in short, is to fulfill our role as God's trustee. By fulfilling our role as God's trustee we are in fact reminding ourselves of who we are and why we are here and what lies beyond this transient life. There can be no better reminder for humankind as we enter the third millennium.

Chandra Muzaffar
President, International Movement for a Just World, Malaysia

I believe that as we stand on the threshold of the third millennium, we see signs of humanity's awakening from the story of a clockwork universe set in motion by its creator and left to run down as its spring unwinds. This deadly tale led us to believe that life is an accident and consciousness an illusion.

It caused us to forget the loving story of a living cosmos striving to know itself through an eternal process of transcendence toward ever higher levels of complexity and consciousness. We now are reawakening to the truth that life is integral to creation and that consciousness is integral to its purpose. This in turn awakens us to possibilities for intelligent, self-aware living and the creation of new forms of social organization grounded in our capacities for cooperation and compassion in service to the whole.

287

David C. Korten
Chairman, The Positive Futures Network, Washington State

We used to pray for wine, flour, oil.
We knew the deal:
We pleased You and asked for the things we needed.
We expected You would come through.

I still need wine, flour (white and wheat), oil (olive and
    canola),
But I do not ask for them (the market is down the road, and I
    drive).

This does not mean You are off the hook.
As I see it, the deal stands:
My pleasing You, my asking for what I cannot get alone.
Love, health, protection, love.

Mi-ma'ahmakim, kir-ticha Yah
From my depths I call to you:

Give me the courage to call out to You for what I need;
I need you to be ready to hear me.

Vanessa L. Ochs
Senior Fellow, National Jewish Center
for Learning and Leadership, New York

I've been to thousands of meetings over the years. Many have a gloomy tone to them. And there's a reason. Typical meetings focus on bad situations, sometimes very bad ones, and on problems—*hard* problems, meaning structural problems, meaning long-term problems, so they're not going to be easy to deal with. You might chip away at them. But they're going to be really hard to resolve in a serious fashion.

It obviously makes sense to concentrate on the problems that lie ahead, and not on the achievements that have been finally reached. But that can lead to a kind of paralyzing despair that "things are hopeless so why even bother to try?" This is morally wrong, and also analytically wrong, and historically wrong.

If you look at history, even recent history, you see that there is indeed progress. The world is a better place than it was even a few years ago. There are victories and they are cumulative. And there is also regression. So it is not straight progress by any means; there are plenty of defeats and periods of regression. We happen to be in a regression period at the moment, but by no means the first one.

However, over time the cycle I think is clearly, generally upwards. And it doesn't happen by laws of nature. And it doesn't happen by social laws (assuming that there are any; it's not always so obvious). It happens as the result of hard work by dedicated people who are willing to look at problems honestly, to try to figure out what they're about, to look at them without illusions, and to go to work chipping away at them, with no guarantee of success—in fact, with a need for a rather high tolerance for failure along the way, and plenty of disappointments.

Noam Chomsky
Political commentator, author, Massachusetts

Reflections on Politics, Economics, and Morality

The preamble to the U.S. Constitution declares that one of that document's purposes is to secure "the blessings of liberty, to ourselves and our posterity." Shouldn't those blessings include air fit to breathe, water decent enough to drink, and land as beautiful for our descendants as it was for our ancestors?

We need a Seventh Generation Amendment to the U.S. Constitution to protect our common-property rights and ensure these blessings to ourselves and our posterity.

Common-property resources are those that are not or cannot be owned by an individual or a corporation, but are held by all people. These "blessings of liberty" should be used or enjoyed only in ways that do not impair the rights of others—including future generations—to use or enjoy them. This is perhaps best reflected in the Iroquois Confederacy's maxim: "In our every deliberation, we must consider the impact of our decisions on the next seven generations."

The rights of all people to use and enjoy air, water, and common lands are essential to life, liberty, and the pursuit of happiness. These most basic human rights have been impaired by those who discharge toxic substances into the air or water, and by those who extract resources from public lands with little concern for fellow citizens or future generations. Their actions imperil our lives, our liberty, and our ability to pursue happiness. Such actions must be recognized as fundamentally wrong in our system of laws, just as the theft or destruction of private property is fundamentally wrong. . . .

The Fifth Amendment preserves our right to private property and the protection of that property. The U.S. legal system needs to establish a clear distinction between private property and common property. Both must be defended vigorously. If private property has found a safe haven in the Fifth Amendment, where is common property equally protected?

Our proposed Seventh Generation Amendment to the U.S. Constitution states: *The right of citizens of the United States to use and enjoy air, water, sunlight, and other renewable resources determined by the Congress to be common property shall not be impaired, nor shall such use impair their availability for the use of future generations.*

Those who framed the Constitution could not have imagined the United States as it is at the millennium. If we don't think of the generations to come, there may not be a United States to imagine.

Winona LaDuke
Mississippi Band Anishinabe, Honor the Earth, Minnesota

*   *   *

Brothers, we now turn our faces toward the future and continue to wish you well in your endeavors as a nation. Perhaps it would be well for you to look back again at our principles of peace, justice, and equality, to grasp firmly our hands in recognition of our long association, and to heed the treaties that were made so long ago—that these treaties may thrive for our posterity as we walk down the long journey to eternity and we continue our association as government to government.

Chief Oren Lyons
"Speech to the U.S. Senate," Iroquois Nation, New York

Thank you, God, for letting me be alive at this moment.

What a wonderful moment for renewal of that which is best in all of humanity! What a blessing to be alive when the peoples of the world momentarily allow ourselves to reconnect to the deepest spiritual truths we know, AND allow ourselves to feel our mutual interdependence and need for each other's love and recognition, compassion, and understanding.

292

How wonderful to know: that the universe itself is permeated by an unending love, that the ultimate power of the universe is the Power of Healing and Transformation, YHWH—the force that we Jews call God or the Eternal or the Ultimate Reality—and that this Power is a power of goodness, a power that flows through each of us and makes possible our role as healers and transformers of the planet in partnership with the ultimate Transformer.

Yet I can't fully be here in this moment without acknowledging that spiritual celebrations, and even articulations of glorious visions of transformation, are sometimes used as ways to avoid the actual suffering in the world and the ways that we contribute to that suffering. The risk of celebration that does not simultaneously seek to rein in the power of multinational corporations, or that does not challenge the ethos of the materialism and selfishness that are the inevitable outgrowths of the logic of the international competitive marketplace, is that it may confirm us in paths of narcissistic self-indulgence in which our ceremonial references to the poor replace actual social struggle to eliminate poverty, homelessness, hunger, and disease. Let us reject cynicism about the possibility of building a very different kind of world—a world in which ethical and spiritual behavior become the norm. Let us agree that in the coming years we will insist on a "new bottom line" of love and solidarity and spiritual sensitivity, so that every institution and social practice is deemed "productive" to the extent that it maximizes our capacities to be loving, caring, and ethically/spiritually/ecologically alive and aware.

Joyfully responding to the glory of this universe, humbled by our responsibility to save it from ecological destruction and moral and spiritual degradation, forgiving each other for the numerous ways that we have failed to be adequately nurturing, we enter into the coming period affirming goodness, hope, and possibility, affirming pleasure, affirming life itself, and affirming our commitment to be partners with God in *Tikkun*, the healing and transformation of the universe.

Rabbi Michael Lerner
Editor, Tikkun magazine, California

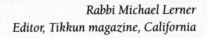

We believe that Life is the most precious possession.

We believe that we ought to mobilize all life forces against the forces of death.

We believe that mutual understanding will bring us to mutual cooperation; and this mutual cooperation will bring peace; and this peace is the road to humankind's survival.

We believe natural resources ought to be preserved, not depleted; for they are the inheritance of our children.

We believe that the polluting of our air, water, and land ought to stop; they are the basic necessities of life.

We believe that plant life ought to be preserved: herbs that appeared 50 million years ago; majestic trees from 20 million years ago; preparing our planet for human life.

We believe that our source of sustenance ought to be fresh, pure, natural, without chemical products or artificial processes.

We believe in the simple life, natural, creative, absorbing all energy sources, harmony and awareness.

We believe that improving human life on the planet begins with individual efforts; we are all parts of a whole, and each part can be said to contain the whole.

We believe in God the Father, Mother Nature, and in the Human Family.

Miguel Grinberg
Poet, journalist, and ecologist,
recipient of Global 500 Award, Argentina
Translated by Joseph Richey

Reflections on Politics, Economics, and Morality

May we as a nation be guided by the Divine to rediscover the sacred flame of our national heritage, which so many have given their lives to safeguard.

Let the wounds of separation and division be healed by opening our hearts to listen to the truth on all sides, allowing us to find a higher truth that includes us all.

May we learn to honor and enjoy our diversity and differences as a people, even as we more deeply touch our fundamental unity.

May we as a people undergo a transformation that will draw forth individuals to lead our nation who embody courage, compassion, and a higher vision.

May our leaders inspire us, and we so inspire each other with our potential that a new spirit of forgiveness, caring, and honesty be born in our nation.

May we as a united people move with clear, directed purpose to take our place within the community of nations and help build a better future for all humanity.

May we as a nation rededicate ourselves to truly living as one nation, under God, indivisible, with liberty and justice for all.

Corinne McLaughlin and Gordon Davidson
The Center for Visionary Leadership, Washington, D.C.

Part 9

PARABLES *of* OUR TIME

Stories hold, in their narrative layers,
the sedimented knowledge accumulated by our
progenitors.

DAVID ABRAM

There is a story told by the farmer-poet Wendell Berry of an old bucket that had been hanging on a fencepost near his farm for something like fifty years. He remembers hearing a story about it when he was a boy. That story told of how the black hired hands on his grandfather's farm had looked for something to cook their eggs in during one lunchbreak. They found and used a bucket that had once held tar, and one of the eggs turned black in cooking. The men joked heartily about who would eat the "black" egg—so the story was told. When Berry took notice of the old bucket on the fencepost as an adult, it still showed dry scales of tar inside.

The bucket also held the accumulation of a half-century of leaves, insects, and bird and mouse droppings, which—through what Berry calls "the chief work of the world"—had produced several inches of black humus in the bottom of the bucket. This essential process of soil-making has been at work for countless millennia over most of the land surface of the world. Without it we would perish. Berry draws a lesson from this simple parable: like the bucket, "a human community, too, must collect leaves and stories, and turn them to account. It must build soil, and build that memory of itself—in lore and story and song—that will be its culture.... A human community, if it is to last long, must exert a sort of centripetal force, holding local soil and local memory in place. Practically speaking, human society has no work more important than this."

This section of stories is like that bucket—a small part of the immense work of the world to remember and restore the collective ground of our being. Of course, Berry's bucket also holds real soil and not just stories, and his emphasis on the work of the local community to nurture its local soil, as well as its memory, is crucial.

We repeat Berry's story here so that we can understand the parable of the bucket in terms of the gift of story to the evolution of the human community's identity. While stories everywhere arise from specific places and traditions, in the context of this "bucket"—Part 9—the stories here speak also to the "trans-local community" of our species—the deepening recognition within diverse cultures of what constitutes the kinship ties of the human family. These little stories and parables are representative of the accumulating compost of tales that extend our various identities as people of a certain place and background to include our common identity as children of the same earth. This is not to say that the diversity of cultures should blend into one, becoming a kind of global cultural mush; such a project would be boring. The place-specific and culture-specific diversity of these and all good stories is the source of their authenticity and power. What touches us here is the open-hearted inclusion of what we might call the "other" into our sense of who we are. A passage from Rabbi Rami Shapiro's story illustrates this well:

And God was saddened by the false divisions. So God called all the people together and stood them in a great

---

valley. God called each person to stand before a divine mirror in which each person saw reflected not her own image, but the images of everyone else.

Of course, the theme of humankind's kinship ties is not new to our time; it is probably as old as storytelling itself. As generation has followed generation, the spiritual guides, prophets, and teachers of our ancestors have honored these deeper kinship ties that unite us beyond the immediate bonds of our tribe. And we will probably always need to be reminded of them, given our tendency to distrust those who appear different from us. Over the millennia, reminders such as these have passed from people to people and generation to generation, gradually accumulating, like the dark humus in that bucket, the fertile belief in our common humanity.

By the end of the longest day of the year he could not stand it,
he went up the iron stairs through the roof of the building
and over the soft, tarry surface
to the edge, put one leg over the complex green tin cornice
and said if they came a step closer that was it.
Then the huge machinery of the earth began to work for his
     life,

302

the cops came in their suits blue-gray as the sky on a cloudy
     evening,
and one put on a bullet-proof vest, a
black shell around his own life,
life of his children's father, in case
the man was armed, and one, slung with a
rope like the sign of his bounden duty,
came up out of a hole in the top of the neighboring building
like the gold hole they say is in the top of the head,
and began to lurk toward the man who wanted to die.
The tallest cop approached him directly,
softly slowly, talking to him, talking, talking,
while the man's leg hung over the lip of the next world
and the crowd gathered in the street, silent, and the
hairy net with its implacable grid was
unfolded near the curb and spread out and
stretched as the sheet is prepared to receive at a birth.
Then they all came a little closer
where he squatted next to his death, his shirt
glowing its milky glow like something
growing in a dish at night in the dark in a lab and then
everything stopped
as his body jerked and he

Parables of Our Time

stepped down from the parapet and went toward them
and they closed on him, I thought they were going to
beat him up, as a mother whose child has been
lost will scream at the child when it's found, they
took him by the arms and held him up and
leaned him against the wall of the chimney and the
tall cop lit a cigarette
in his own mouth, and gave it to him, and
then they all lit cigarettes, and the
red, glowing ends burned like the
tiny campfires we lit at night
back at the beginning of the world.

303

Sharon Olds
Poet, New York

In May 1992, during the siege of Sarajevo, a mortar shell exploded at 4:00 P.M. outside a bakery in the city where a long line of people had lined up to buy bread. Twenty-two people were killed and hundreds wounded in the explosion.

But despite the danger, the next day hungry people once again lined up to get bread, so desperate were their lives. Yet this day was different, for at 4:00 P.M. Vedran Smailovic, the principal cellist of the Sarajevo Opera, arrived in front of the bakery carrying a chair and his cello. Dressed in a formal black suit and white tie, he sat down and played the mournful Adagio by Albinoni. And for the next twenty-one days, Smailovic came to the street in front of the bakery and played the Adagio.

The passion of this act, the power of the music, brought hope and determination to the besieged city. And since that time Vedran Smailovic's example has inspired others—in Seattle, in Washington, D.C. (during the inaugural activities of President Clinton), at the Cathedral of St. John the Divine in New York City. Smailovic played the Adagio at the Statue of Liberty commemorating the one thousandth day of the siege of Sarajevo; he performed in Belfast in 1998 prior to the signing of the peace accord for Northern Ireland. Yo Yo Ma played David Wilde's "The Cellist of Sarajevo" at the International Cello Festival in Manchester, England, in 1994, with Smailovic in the audience.

And so that audacious act of faith and passion on the streets of Sarajevo continues to inspire and challenge us to witness to the light within that will not be extinguished. As we move into this new millennium, the cellist Vedran Smailovic inspires us to live a hopeful future into being.

Richard Deats
Editor, Fellowship magazine,
Fellowship of Reconciliation, New York

Parables of Our Time

At a recent conference, I asked one thousand people,

"If you had only twenty-four hours left to live, where would you spend it? How would you spend it, and who (if anyone) would you have with you?"

When I read their answers on small slips of paper, not one person said, "I will watch TV; I will sit in front of the computer; I will sit in traffic for hours in my car; I will fight with those who don't see things my way; I will go shopping; I will figure out how to make more money." Not one said, "I will stay indoors; I will just go to sleep; I will worry about my hair and my weight; I will not be good to myself and those around me."

Instead, the thousand slips of paper spoke of loving family and friends, being in the most beautiful places on earth, making peace with all beings (especially those we have needlessly harmed), waking up, and spreading as much peace and laughter and honesty and touch as possible in those last hours.

I laughed and cried and smiled as I read the answers. I realized then that going into the next millennium, we should live as if this were our last twenty-four hours, choosing the most honest and loving way at every moment. Perhaps the way to do this is to live the golden rule: do unto others (all living beings) as you would have done unto you; do not do unto others that which you would not want done unto you.

With this choice of loving and caring, our twenty-four hours will repeat itself day after day, week after week, year after year, decade after decade.

Rae Sikora
Co-founder, Center for Compassionate Living, Maine

Born on the Dutch-Belgian border, I was five years old when in 1914—half a mile from our doorstep—World War I exploded. The barbaric twentieth century had started in earnest. If I am still around on December 31, 1999, I will have survived it in its entirety. Astonishing.

I grew up on a tiny agnostic family island in the ocean of a thoroughly Catholic culture, was still very small when I saw people cross themselves when a funeral passed by. It touched me to the core.

At moments of crisis, of being overwhelmed by unbearable beauty, joy, terrible compassion, I traced the gesture in secret over my heart, under my jacket. It became my only prayer, wordless. It evoked a Presence, undefined. Its upright linked heaven and earth; the horizontal embraced all that lives and must die—humans, animals, trees. The human face itself mirrored the sign: nose vertical, eyes horizontal.

Now, eight decades later, forever refusing to label myself a *this* or a *that,* still allergic to all affiliations, it happens at moments of deep emotion, of wonder at being here at all, for once not taking the Mystery of Existing for granted, that I feel my hand moving from forehead to navel, from shoulder to shoulder, still mute, neither petition nor incantation, nor magic, just a hand seeking to touch, to confirm the Presence, the Buddha Nature, the Indwelling Spirit, my only true identity—core of the humanness we share. The Sign, so profaned by centuries of pyres, witch hunts, pogroms has become trans-religious, Sign of the Human, Sign of the Tao, which, Lao Tzu said, cannot be divided, but must be shared.

On New Year 2000—if I'm still around—the mute Sign will be my prayer for our species' survival as a still-Human species, and that of the good earth that spawned us.

Frederick Franck
Artist and author, Pacem in Terris, New York

*   *   *

Late one afternoon four years ago, I took the Venerable Maha Ghosananda, recognized as the senior Buddhist monk of Cambodia, to tea at the coffee shop in the lobby of the Imperial Hotel in New Delhi.

I knew that in the previous year he had been part of the delegation that had walked through the gates of Auschwitz on the fiftieth anniversary of the liberation of that concentration camp and had walked into Hiroshima six months later on the fiftieth anniversary of the first explosion of an atomic bomb on a human population.

I said, "What are you doing now?"

He said, "I'm trying very hard to get an international ban against land mines. In Cambodia every day many people are killed or maimed from stepping on land mines."

"What can I do to help?" I asked.

He said, "You can ask everyone you meet to sign a petition against land mines." And he reached into the sleeve of his orange robe, withdrew a petition, and handed it to me.

May we all be not more than one sleeve-length away from connecting our commitment to a peaceful heart to our commitment to a peaceful world.

Sylvia Boorstein
Buddhist teacher, Spirit Rock Center, California

"You know what I really think? I really think that one day the world will be great, I really believe the world gonna be great one day."

The man who said that was Cesar Chavez, a migrant farm worker, and a black man. Cesar shared this astonishing hope of an evolution in human values, and I do too; it is the only hope we have.

Before this century is done, there will be an evolution in our values and the values of human society, not because we have become more civilized but because, on a blighted earth, we will have no choice. This evolution—actually a revolution whose violence will depend on the violence with which it is met—must aim at an order of things that treats us and our habitat with respect.

I think often of the visit Cesar and I made to the archdiocese on a summer day in San Francisco, and the way Cesar vanished into the cold modern house of God, so unlike the simple missions he prefers. An elevator must have rushed him to the top, because moments later there came a rapping from on high, and Cesar appeared in silhouette behind the panes, waving and beckoning from the silences of sun and glass like a man trapped against his will in Heaven. His dance of woe was a pantomime of man's fate, and this transcendental clowning, this impossible gaiety, which illuminated even his most desperate moments, was his most moving trait. Months later I would still see that human figure in the glittering high windows of the twentieth century. The hands, the dance, cried to the world: Wait! Have faith! Look, look! Let's go! Good-bye! Hello! I love you!

Peter Matthiessen
Author, New York

We often find peace and preserve it or develop a nonviolent attitude and take comfort for ourselves; but according to my grandfather, Mohandas Karamchand Gandhi, all of this is meaningless if we don't share it.

To illustrate his point, he told me a story of a king who ruled in ancient India. He was concerned about the meaning of peace and searched for the answer diligently, but no one could satisfy his curiosity. Someone told him: "There is a wise man living at the edge of town. Why don't you ask him?"

The king went to the wise old man and asked him the eternal question. The philosopher quietly went into his kitchen and brought a grain of wheat and placed it in the palm of the king and said: "Here is your answer."

The king was puzzled but too proud to display his ignorance so, clutching the grain in his palm, he went back to the palace, got a nice gold box, placed the grain in it, and locked the box in the safe. Every morning he opened the box and examined the grain of wheat and found no change nor any answers.

Several weeks later, the king explained his dilemma to another visiting wise man: "I don't know what it means. The grain hasn't changed, and it's provided me with no answers to the question, What is the meaning of peace?"

The wise one said: "If you keep the grain of wheat in a gold box, it will rot and disintegrate. But if you plant and nurture it, the grain will sprout and multiply until you have a whole field of wheat." Similarly, unless peace and nonviolence are allowed to interact with all the right elements, they won't mean much to anyone.

Arun Gandhi
Founder and director, M. K. Gandhi Institute
for Nonviolence, Tennessee

Rabbi Yerachmiel gathered the children of the village to him.

"Listen, children, listen. For a great mystery is about to be revealed to you.

"In the beginning, God made a single human from the dust of the earth. This one was red, yellow, brown, black, and white, for all the sands of creation were used to fashion it. Male and female, it was, for God had not yet separated the sexes. And God said: This one is in My Image, for this one includes all creation in one being.

"God had thought this being would be happy, but it was not happy. It was lonely. So God divided the one human in two, female and male. And then these two divided themselves even further until the unity of the first person was lost in the divisions created by the many people who followed.

"And God was saddened by the false divisions. So God called all the people together and stood them in a great valley. God called each person to stand before a divine mirror in which each person saw reflected not her own image, but the images of everyone else.

"Many people were frightened by the strange mirror, and ran away to hide. But others understood that God was reminding them of their unity. And these people set for themselves a great task: to help each of us see the whole world reflected in each face. God helped them. God took the great mirror and made millions upon millions of tiny mirrors. God placed these tiny mirrors in the eyes of every human being, even you and me, so that if you look in another's eyes you will see reflected there the whole world and the One who created it.

"You are the children of those daring few, and it is time for you to carry on their work: to learn to look into the eyes of another and see the whole world and the One from Whom the whole world flows. If you fail, if you see only yourself reflected in God's mirror, the lie you will live will burn the world to a cinder. The whole world is waiting for you, my children. You must see the truth and proclaim it. You must open your eyes and see."

And the children looked at each other in awe. Some saw and smiled. Some saw and cried. Some could not see at all. But all held tight, one to the other, and God sighed a great sigh of hope.

Rabbi Rami M. Shapiro
Florida

There is a language older by far and deeper than words. It is the language of bodies, of body on body, wind on snow, rain on trees, wave on stone. It is the language of dream, of gesture, of symbol, of memory. We have forgotten this language, forgotten it for so long we do not even remember that it exists. If we are to survive, we must again remember this language. We must relearn how to think like the planet.

I remember walking into a cold January afternoon several years ago. My breath hung white in the air, and two dogs danced at my feet. I heard in the distance the clamor of geese, then stood speechless to watch a huge V fly low overhead. I opened my mouth to say something—I didn't know what it would be—and heard my voice say three times, "Godspeed." Suddenly, and for no reason I could understand, I burst into tears. Then I ran into the house.

Walking back outside later and staring into the now empty sky, I realized that in speaking not only had I been wishing the geese well for their journey south but they had been using my voice and my breath to wish me just-as-well on my own just-as-difficult journey—this journey of opposition to the culture that is destroying life on the planet. The tears, it came clear to me, had been neither from sorrow nor joy, but from homecoming, like a sailor who has been too long at sea, and who spontaneously bursts into sobs on feeling those tentative first steps back on solid ground, back at home.

If we are to survive, we need the planet's help, just as it needs ours. To dismantle the walls we've so laboriously constructed to constrict our broken hearts, we must step away from our isolation from the rest of the world. There is a whole world waiting for us, ready to welcome us home. They have missed us as sorely as we have missed them. It is time. Return.

Godspeed.

Derrick Jensen
Environmentalist, California

*   *   *

When the Creator created the people to be the forebears of the Sami, he knew about the hardships their descendants would endure—small in number, spread over a vast area, victimized by exploitation, colonization, assimilation, and self-degradation.

The myth which no one ever has dared to test, tells us that the Great Creator took a living and beating heart of a two-year-old reindeer cow and put it at the center of the earth, so every time we Sami feel our existence threatened or fear for the future, we just put our ears to the ground to listen for the heartbeats from below.

If the heart is still beating, there is a future for the people. The beating of the reindeer heart deep down below reverberates in the sound of the drum, driving us to sing and dance and rejoice, as long as the reindeer graze, the moss grows, and people believe there is a heart beating for everyone at the center of the earth.

Harald Gaski
Sami of Norway

We began as creatures in a garden, married to it and to each other. The marriage was made in heaven. It left us nothing to desire, no end to life beyond the living of it.

Other omnivores shared the garden with us. None of them had an appetite like ours, because none had an imagination. We swallowed them. Hunger of imagination ate us out of garden after garden; out of cave, cottage, and city; out of ancestral house and earthly home. Only infinity could appease us, so we invented transcendence, universal unity. Along the way, we filed for divorce. We aimed at heaven, an end beyond life.

In a way, we got there. Hunger of imagination took us up and out, into space. We swallowed it. Its uninhabitable, undifferentiated immensity inhabited us. Then we lived in modules, in capsules; we breathed an artificial air. We had graduated from the endless practice of nature into pure theory. Our bodies became luggage we did not need, scaffolding that had served its purpose. There was no up, no down—no gravity, friction, or index of time.

From here, in the great void that desire has brought us to, something wakens in us. Is it a dream? First, there are shards and fragments, an untidy midden, faded snapshots. Here are horses, thudding, shifting, and actual in the prehistoric half-light of a stable. Here are fish, teeming upriver when the shad-bush blooms. Here are figured rites for seasons, celebrations for nativities, flowers for the grave. Imagination turns to memory. It hungers for finitude, for necessity, for growing old. Its light hallows the palpable, the ordinary, the recurrent.

The lovers it sees leaning toward each other are not young, are not innocent. Its prayer for them is modest because it is also desperate: may they reunite without fanfare; may they keep house together again; be body and soul, separate and inseparable once more.

Franklin Burroughs
Professor of English, Bowdoin College, Maine

*   *   *

YAHWEH: Early this morning, Urset, when you walked along Frijoles Creek, what was it I heard you say?

URSET: I said: The morning is crisp and bright. I expect something to define the air momentarily, perhaps the shrill cry of a rabbit or a wren. The water of Frijoles Creek runs southward through splinters of light and patterns of shade. It runs without urgency, as I walk. It keeps the faster pace, but it and I proceed steadily, like the pilgrims of Chimayo, in our natures and in one nature, to the edge of the world. I hear among the stony churns of the creek words that I heard from an old man when I was young, *"Muy bonita dia!"* Our laughter, his and mine, roves upon the cliffs of tuff close by. It is the first of all mornings, and it is unspeakably old.

YAHWEH: Amen.

N. Scott Momaday
Author, educator, and artist, Kiowa Nation, New Mexico

316

We've been reading it wrong.
It's a story of how we took
nature down with us all right,
but not because we're such
important hot shots that what
we decide goes for everybody,
or the Creator is such an abusive
s.o.b. that he punishes the innocent
for the crimes of the guilty if
the guilty are godly enough.
We are a twisted species.
We bend our view of the universe
around ourselves as center cog.
By our distortion we have injured Eden.
We haven't a clue.

Complexity grants that the least
significant events or choices
affect everything to infinity—
microbes on pear trees, and
the honey bee as well as
human beings.

Our infant species dreamed it was
above its elders, beyond its betters,
the high-chair tyrant entitled to rule
the rest, and worse—granted this
by a god. We named the others and
proclaimed them Other, ourselves
what counts, holier than them.

We threw ourselves out of Eden.
Injured by us but alive,
it's still here all around us.
We have only to return to our senses,
wake from our hubris, sit down
with our creature kin and humbly ask
by what name each knows itself,
and listen, without denial or defense,
for the names they have been saving up
to call us.

317

Once that's over we can negotiate
everything and start again
with what's left.
Then—
                In the beginning . . .

                The Rev. Alla Renée Bozarth
                Poet and priest, Wisdom House, Oregon

In the beginning was the gift. And the gift was with God and the gift was God. And the gift came and set its tent among us, first in the form of a fireball that burned unabated for 750,000 years and cooked in its immensely hot oven hadrons and leptons.

These gifts found a modicum of stability—enough to give birth to the first atomic creatures, hydrogen and helium. A billion years of stewing and stirring and the gifts birthed galaxies—spinning, whirling, living galaxies—created trillions of stars, lights in the heavens and cosmic furnaces that made more gifts through violent explosions of vast supernovas burning bright with the glow of more than a billion stars.

Gifts upon gifts, gifts birthing gifts, gifts exploding, gifts imploding, gifts of light, gifts of darkness. Cosmic gifts and subatomic gifts. All drifting and swirling, being born and dying, in some vast secret of a plan. Which was also a gift.

One of these supernovas exploded in a special manner, sending a unique gift to the universe, which later-coming creatures would one day call earth, their home. Its biosphere was a gift, wrapping it with beauty and dignity and just the right protection from sun's radiation and from the cosmic cold. And eternal night. This gifted planet was set as a jewel in its most exquisite setting, the exact distance of 100 million miles from its mother star, the sun.

New gifts arose, never seen in such forms in the universe—rocks, oceans, continents, multicellular creatures that moved by their own inner power. Life was born! Gifts that had taken the form of fireball and helium, galaxies and stars, rock and water, now took the form of Life! Life—new gift of the universe. Flowers of multiple color and scent, trees standing upright. Forests arose offering places for all manner of creeping, crawling things, things that fly and sing, things that swim and slither, things that run on four legs, and, eventually, things that stand and walk on two. With thumbs that move to make still more creativity—more gift-making—possible.

The human became a gift, but also a danger, for its powers of creativity were unique in their potential for destruction or healing. How would humans use these gifts? Which direction would they choose? The earth waited for an answer to these questions, and is still waiting, trembling.

Teachers were sent, divine incarnations birthed from the soil. Isis and Hesiod, Buddha and Lao Tzu, Moses and Isaiah, Sarah and Esther, Jesus and Paul, Mary and Hildegard, Chief Seattle and Buffalo Woman, to teach the humans ways of compassion—and still the earth waits to see if humanity was gift or curse.

Have you ever given a gift and then regretted it afterward? Earth wonders and waits. For the gift has been made flesh and dwells everywhere among us and we tend to know it not. And to treat it not as a gift but as an object. To be used, abused, trampled underfoot—even crucified. But to those who do receive it as a gift all is promised. All shall be called children of the gift, sons and daughters of grace. For all generations.

Matthew Fox
Author and teacher, University of Creation Spirituality,
California

After hiking eleven miles along mountain ridge paths, I arrive back in the village of Colares; weary, hungry. Immediately I head for the local bakery for a warm loaf of *terra da pao,* the Portuguese bread of the earth. The baker has flecks of flour on her hands as she wraps the bread in newspaper. Her weariness is leavened with pride. When she offers the small package to me, the heat of the bread rises in waves to warm my chilled hands.

With this gift in hand, I hurry down past the medieval stone pillory where villagers were publicly scorned during the Inquisition, and beyond the outdoor cafe where the locals vehemently argue the rural politics of Portugal, to the cobbled road that will take me home. Along the way I break off pieces of bread to fortify myself. I taste wheat, millstone, rain, sun, and the paths left by the baker's kneading fingers. I savor the passion that binds together farmer, harvester, and baker.

Beyond the village is a narrow flagstoned path that meanders through fields of sunflowers. Still savoring the bread, I ride a carousel of memory taste: pumpernickel in Russia, soda bread in Ireland, holy bread in Israel, *pandesol* in the Philippines, oak-fired sourdough on the rue du Cherch-Midi in Paris, and the loaf of carbonized bread in front of the baker's oven at Pompeii.

Twisting the crust in my fingers, I marvel at the mystery of dough, and the smell of woodsmoke, and the sound of the oven's hymn of bread.

In this brief curve of time, I realize that if I am not grateful here and now, I will never know what the wise poet meant when he chewed his words carefully, as if they were hot and freshly baked from an ancient stone oven, and said, I like reality: it tastes of bread.

Phil Cousineau
Author, California

Parables of Our Time

To my great-great-grandchildren—seven generations into the future:

I am writing from the last moments of the twentieth century, sending this message to my future from your past. I hope this letter reaches you and that you are in good health, surrounded by the kindness our Earth Mother and all her family continually bestow. You may have heard my name, as the history has been recounted in your lodges, of a time when the voice of the sacred waterdrum sounded at the Eastern door after generations of silence. Amidst the din and confusion of our troubled time when all was thought to be lost, there was one listener who had not forgotten the Creator's dream—Bawdwaywidun, who heard the calling of the drum that would lead us into the promised time of the Seventh Fire. I was the one upon whose lap the drum was placed—the drum that opened the door of the lodge that was revived again in our time. I send this message from that time—from the dawning of the Seventh Fire.

As I look back to my grandfathers before me, I can see they have held me in their thoughts while they struggled to deal with the circumstances of their time. It was seven generations ago from where I am now, during those dark days of the Sixth Fire, that the great Chief Tecumseh gathered the people of many Nations together to try to curb the unending invasion of our lands and our way of life. Tecumseh and other leaders sent ahead to us a spirit of determination, of unity, of love for the land and our spiritual ways. From out of a time when all seemed hopeless, he gave us the greatest hope—hope in ourselves and in the resilience of the Anishinabe spirit.

As you look back on what is "history" to you now, it must deeply puzzle you how we could have almost totally abandoned what was given to us by the Creator. How we could have allowed our language to almost disappear. How we could have let our songs become silent and our memories unable to recall our sacred beginnings. How we could have exchanged the depth and beauty of our teachings for a way of life and belief that was so shallow and so destructive of the Creation and of the human spirit.

The good news I send to you is that we have been awakened from this sleep. The voice of the drum we call the "Little Boy" has been heard and has called us out of our confusion and our forgetfulness to see the beautiful future ahead of us. Tobacco smoke, once again, carries our words to the spirit of truth, love, and peace. The sacred songs are heard again and are echoed by our young people and our children. The renewed knowledge of the prophecies has connected us to the unbroken strings of lives of the generations of Anishinabe before us. And the lodge of life has been seen stretching into the future to include you in our dreams and in our songs.

Our prophecies tell us that after that long period of time where the devastating events of the Fifth and Sixth Fires cast a long shadow over our land, our people, and our lives, a new generation, a new people would emerge. This new generation would retrace their steps, to seek out and gather together what had been lost, forgotten, and left scattered along the trail of the past. We are those "new ones," and we are reassembling the "bundle" that had been left behind. The contents of this bundle is our legacy, our gift to you—our future.

This bundle holds our language, our teachings, our songs, and all the finest expressions of our creative spirit. These have been gathered from the past and revived again to inspire us, guide us, and lead us in our time. At the very center of this bundle is the spirit, for the spirit is the "life-force" that makes everything want to live. The spirit only knows kindness and eternally yearns for harmony and peace and love. The spirit treasures every moment of its sojourn here and delights and takes even gleeful joy in being in and enlivening this world.

The spirit looks forward to living every day in this world
    loves the rhythmic mother's heartbeat inside the womb
    cherishes the trickling, flowing, surging sound
    of bloodstreams coursing through arteries and veins
    as Earth Mother does of rivers and streams and brooks
    rushing above and below the surface of the ground.

The spirit delights in the vibrancy and resilience of flesh and
        bone
    revels in the feeling of physical life
    through the many fingers that touch the world
    enjoys the wonders of human eyes
    that see every color of every miracle of life's unfolding.

The spirit marvels at the mind's ability to imagine
    to make concepts of seed thoughts
    to ponder and to dream.

The spirit likes to send a message in the wind
    likes to sing songs through the bubbling flow of water
        over rocks
    likes to feel the emotions of the heart
    likes to shape its rhythm into dancing feet
    likes to make sounds and images, colors and sensations
    into ideas and visions not yet dreamed.

Know that the spirit is a special gift to life. But also know that this seeing, hearing, touching, tasting physical life of sight and sound, sensation and passion is a living, cherished, and precious gift to the spirit.

My grandchildren: our greatest gift to you is that we have touched the spirit; we have found the heart and the heart is filled with kindness. In our future, in your time, we will be the "spirits" of your past generations, with the memories of life lived. As you remember us, as you prepare to feast us in your lodge:

sing our beautiful songs
    so that we might dance to their melody in the skyworld
give voice to our most sacred teachings
    so that we might hear the knowledge of the starworld
savor the deepest love of life
    so that we might feel the throb at the heart of the universe
love and cherish your relatives around you
    so that we might sense, too, the embrace of loved ones
and when you touch life, touch it deeply
    so that we will feel through your fingertips
    the memories of the beautiful earth.

We promise to keep alive for you the beauty of our language. We will do everything to ensure that you will have a beautiful home upon our Mother, surrounded by our earth relatives. We pledge to keep the waters clean so that the forever-life-giving stream will also flow through your life. We will build our future on the foundations of kindness, respect, truth, and peace so that you will have solid ground upon which to build the lodge of your life. As the generations before us have thought of us, we think of you. We have touched the spirit, and the spirit is forever.

All my love to you, my grandchildren of the Eighth Fire from your great-great-grandfather at the dawn of the Seventh Fire.

Onaubinisay (James Dumont)
Waubezhayshee (Marten) Clan, Ojibway-Anishinabe Nation,
Three Fires Midewiwin Lodge, Canada

Part 10

WE *the* PEOPLE

Their strength is in their compassion;
God's light shines through their hearts.
Their children's children will bless them,
And the work of their hands will endure.

PSALM 24 (*translated by*
Stephen Mitchell)

The writings in this final section are collective prayers of the people. They represent a profoundly hopeful gift from the twentieth century to the twenty-first, and beyond. Never before in our history have so many of us come together for the purpose of expressing values that we hold in common. For more than fifty years, many thousands of people from around the world have taken part in articulating these statements. Collectively written and endorsed as declarations and charters for the United Nations, the World Parliament of Religions, the World Conference on Women, and many other collective purposes, these words are the foundation for an emerging global ethic. They have their roots in the great moral teachings of the world's spiritual traditions (both Eastern and Western), in the writings of poets and philosophers over the centuries, and in earlier political covenants in the West, such as the Magna Carta (1215), the English Bill of Rights (1689), the American Declaration of Independence (1776), and the French Declaration of the Rights of Man (1789).

Midway through the twentieth century, as the Second World War raged, Franklin Roosevelt spoke of four freedoms on which world society should be founded: freedom of speech and expression, freedom of religion, freedom from want, and freedom from fear. These freedoms, he stressed, were relevant everywhere in the world on a universal basis. Following the immense suffering of that war and its terrible lessons, the United Nations Charter and then the Universal Declaration of Human Rights sought to express succinctly the norms of basic human rights within a communal context. Hand in hand with the emphasis on individual human rights comes the recognition of the rights of the community. In the words of the U.N. Charter, we must be determined "to practice tolerance and live together in peace with one another as good neighbors."

Upon this foundation, several hundred declarations and treaties have been formulated, over the second half of the twentieth century, dealing with the rights of children, women, indigenous peoples, and all of nature's various life forms. It is as if this great flowering of ethical concerns could come only when we as a species had stared long and hard into the abyss of their negation. Perhaps in this deepening of our moral nature—however incomplete—lies some redemption for the destruction we have inflicted in recent times on each other and the natural world.

One of the most inclusive documents—a work still in progress—is the Earth Charter being developed under the auspices of the United Nations. Its creation, spanning the final decade of the century, has involved consultation with thousands of representatives from every continent. It is an attempt to synthesize our concern for justice and human rights with our recognition of the sacred interdependence of all life. "We must reinvent industrial-technological civilization," the Charter says, "finding new ways to balance self and community, having and being, diversity and unity, short-term and long-term, using and nurturing."

Such exhortations are stirring, but is anybody listening? More important, is anybody *doing?* Without action, the representative documents in Part 10 are only words on paper. It could be argued that the intent of these declarations is ignored in the world as much as it is respected. Yet simply articulating the beliefs contained in these declarations is a critical step in their ultimate realization. As they seek to define international and interfaith norms, values, and ideals, and as we learn to appeal to them when they are ignored or defied, these declarations will increasingly shape and guide our actions.

In this way, these formal statements are prayers—prayers rising up from our collective spirit—stating the obvious, natural yearnings of our hearts that we may, in the words of the Earth Charter, "grow into a family of cultures that allows the potential of all persons to unfold in harmony with the Earth Community."

The Charter of the United Nations, 1945

We the peoples of the United Nations

determined

to save succeeding generations from the scourge of war, which twice in our lifetime has brought untold sorrow to humankind, and to reaffirm faith in fundamental human rights, in the dignity and worth of the human person, in the equal rights of men and women and of nations large and small, and

to establish conditions under which justice and respect for the obligations arising from treaties and other sources of international law can be maintained, and

to promote social progress and better standards of life in larger freedom,

and for these ends

to practice tolerance and live together in peace with one another as good neighbors, and

to unite our strength to maintain international peace and security, and

to ensure, by the acceptance of principles and the institution of methods, that armed force shall not be used, save in the common interest, and

to employ international machinery for the promotion of the economic and social advancement of all peoples,

have resolved to combine our efforts to accomplish these aims.

The Universal Declaration of Human Rights, United Nations, 1948

W*hereas* recognition of the inherent dignity and of the equal and inalienable rights of all members of the human family is the foundation of freedom, justice and peace in the world,

Whereas disregard and contempt for human rights have resulted in barbarous acts which have outraged the conscience of humankind, and the advent of a world in which human beings shall enjoy freedom of speech and belief and freedom from fear and want has been proclaimed as the highest aspiration of the common people,

Whereas it is essential, if men and women are not compelled to have recourse, as a last resort, to rebellion against tyranny and oppression, that human rights should be protected by the rule of law,

Whereas it is essential to promote the development of friendly relations between nations,

Whereas the peoples of the United Nations have in the Charter reaffirmed their faith in fundamental human rights, in the dignity and worth of the human person, and in the equal rights of men and women and have determined to promote social progress and better standards of life in larger freedom,

Whereas Member States have pledged themselves to achieve, in cooperation with the United Nations, the promotion of universal respect for and observance of human rights and fundamental freedoms,

Whereas a common understanding of these rights and freedoms is of the greatest importance for the full realization of this pledge.

Now, therefore, the General Assembly proclaims this Universal Declaration of Human Rights as a common standard of achievement for all peoples and all nations, to the end that every individual and every organ of society, keeping this Declaration constantly in mind, shall strive by teaching and education to promote respect for these rights and freedoms and by progressive measures, national and international, to secure their universal and effective recognition and observance, both among the peoples of Member States themselves and among the peoples of territories under their jurisdiction.

United Nations Declaration
of the Rights of the Child, 1959

Principle One
The child shall enjoy all the rights set forth in this Declaration. All children, without any exception whatsoever, shall be entitled to these rights, without distinction or discrimination on account of race, color, sex, language, religion, political or other opinion, national or social origin, property, birth or other status, whether of himself or of his family.

Principle Two
The child shall enjoy special protection and shall be given opportunities and facilities, by law and by other means, to enable her to develop physically, mentally, morally, spiritually, and socially in a healthy and normal manner and in conditions of freedom and dignity. In the enactment of laws for this purpose the best interests of the child shall be the paramount consideration.

Principle Three
The child shall be entitled from his birth to a name and a nationality.

Principle Four
The child shall enjoy the benefits of social security, she shall be entitled to grow and develop in health; to this end special care and protection shall be provided both to her and to her mother, including adequate pre-natal and post-natal care. The child shall have the right to adequate nutrition, housing, recreation and medical services.

Principle Five

The child who is physically, mentally or socially handicapped shall be given the special treatment, education and care required by his particular condition.

Principle Six

The child, for the full and harmonious development of her personality, needs love and understanding. She shall, wherever possible, grow up in the care and under the responsibility of her parents and in any case in an atmosphere of affection and of moral and material security: a child of tender years shall not, save in exceptional circumstances, be separated from her mother. Society and the public authorities shall have the duty to extend particular care to children without a family and to those without adequate means of support. Payment of state and other assistance toward the maintenance of children of large families is desirable.

Principle Seven

The child is entitled to receive education, which shall be free and compulsory, at least in the elementary stages. He shall be given an education which will promote his general culture, and enable him on a basis of equal opportunity to develop his abilities, his individual judgment, and his sense of moral and social responsibility, and to become a useful member of society.

The best interests of the child shall be the guiding principle of those responsible for his education and guidance; that responsibility lies in the first place with his parents.

The child shall have full opportunity for play and recreation, which should be directed to the same purposes as education; society and the public authorities shall endeavor to promote the enjoyment of this right.

Principle Eight

The child shall in all circumstances be among the first to receive protection and relief.

Principle Nine

The child shall be protected against all forms of neglect, cruelty and exploitation. She shall not be the subject of traffic, in any form.

337

Principle Ten

The child shall be protected from practices which may foster racial, religious and any other form of discrimination. He shall be brought up in a spirit of understanding, tolerance, friendship among peoples, peace and universal friendship and in full consciousness that his energy and talents should be devoted to the service of his fellow men and women.

from
The Kyoto Declaration
World Conference on Religion and Peace, 1970

The World Conference on Religion and Peace represents an historic attempt to bring together men and women of all major religions to discuss the urgent issue of peace. Baha'i, Buddhist, Confucian, Christian, Hindu, Jain, Jew, Muslim, Shintoist, Sikh, Zoroastrian, and others—we have come together in peace out of a common concern for peace.

. . . As we sat down together facing the overriding issues of peace we discovered that the things which unite us are more important than the things which divide us. We found that we share:

A conviction of the fundamental unity of the human family, and the equality and dignity of all human beings;

A sense of the sacredness of the individual person and his conscience;

A sense of the value of human community;

A realization that might is not right; that human power is not self-sufficient and absolute;

A belief that love, compassion, selflessness, and the force of inner truthfulness and of the spirit have ultimately greater power than hate, enmity, and self-interest;

A sense of obligation to stand on the side of the poor and the oppressed as against the rich and the oppressors; and

A profound hope that good will finally prevail.

---

from
The Mount Abu Declaration
presented to the United Nations by
leaders from forty nations, 1989

As a global family we share the same unique planet and share the same hopes and aspirations for a just and humane world. Yet, as we approach the dawn of the next millennium, we are concerned that life on earth is threatened.

Our beautiful planet is faced with a crisis of unprecedented magnitude. In many cultures, the moral fabric of society is challenged by violence, crime, addiction, denial of human rights and human dignity, and the disintegration of family life.

At the same time, we, the people of the world, are yearning for peace and a better world for ourselves and our children. How is it, that with all the human skill and talent that exists, with all the achievements in technology, there is still grinding poverty, massive arms expenditure and a grave deterioration in the environment?

There is so much to be done and so many willing hands and hearts to do it. What is needed is the spirit of co-operation and goodwill, the attitude of love and respect toward each other, the practice of positive and creative thinking, the application of moral and spiritual values in daily life, as well as action based on a shared vision of a better world.

Now is the time to call on the will and the clear vision of the people:

"A vision without a task is but a dream
A task without a vision is drudgery
A vision with a task
can change the world."

We the People

340

We ... [are] people of color, gathered together at this multinational People of Color Environmental Leadership Summit to begin to build a national and international movement of all peoples of color to fight the destruction and taking of our lands and communities, to hereby re-establish our spiritual interdependence to the sacredness of our Mother Earth; to respect and celebrate each of our cultures, languages, and beliefs about the natural world and our roles in healing ourselves; to insure environmental justice; to promote economic alternatives which would contribute to the development of environmentally safe livelihoods; and, to secure our political, economic, and cultural liberation that has been denied for over 500 years of colonization and oppression, resulting in the poisoning of our communities and land and the genocide of our people.

The People's Earth Declaration
International Non-Governmental Organizations Forum,
Rio de Janeiro, 1992

We, the participants of the International Non-Governmental Organizations Forum at the Global Forum '92, have met in Rio de Janeiro as citizens of planet earth to share our concerns, our dreams and our plans for creating a new future for our world. We emerge from these deliberations with a profound sense that in the richness of our diversity, we share a common vision of a human society grounded in the values of simplicity, love, peace and reverence for life and we have achieved a broadly shared consensus that the following principles will guide our continuing collective effort:

The fundamental purpose of economic organization is to meet the community's basic needs, such as for food, shelter, clothing, education, health and the enjoyment of culture. This purpose must take priority over all other forms of consumption, particularly wasteful and destructive forms of consumption such as consumerism and military spending. . . . Other immediate priorities include energy conservation, shifting to reliance on solar energy sources and converting agriculture to sustainable practices that minimize dependence on non-renewable and ecologically harmful inputs.

Beyond meeting basic physical needs, the quality of human life depends more on the development of social relationships, creativity, cultural and artistic expressions, spirituality and opportunity to be a productive member of the community, than on the ever increasing consumption of material goods. Everyone, including the handicapped, must have a full opportunity to participate in all these forms of development.

342

Organizing economic life around decentralized relatively self-reliant local economies that control and manage their own productive resources and have the right to safeguard their own environmental and social standards is essential to sustainability. It strengthens attachments to place, encourages environmental stewardship, enhances local food security, and accommodates distinctive cultural identities. Where the rights and interests of the corporation conflict with the rights and interests of the community, the latter must prevail.

All elements of society, irrespective of gender, class or ethnic identity, have a right and obligation to participate fully in the life and decisions of the community. The presently poor and disenfranchised, in particular, must become full participants. Women's roles, needs, values and wisdom are especially central to decision-making on the fate of the earth. There is an urgent need to involve women at all levels of policy-making, planning and implementation on an equal basis with men. Gender balance is essential to sustainable development. Indigenous peoples also bring vital leadership to the task of conserving the earth and its creatures and in creating a new life-affirming global reality. Indigenous wisdom constitutes one of human society's important and irreplaceable resources. The rights and contributions of indigenous peoples must be recognized.

preamble to

The Declaration on a Global Ethic
The Parliament of the World's Religions, 1993

The world is in agony. The agony is so pervasive and urgent that we are compelled to name its manifestations so that the depth of this pain may be made clear.

343

Peace eludes us; . . . the planet is being destroyed; . . . neighbors live in fear; . . . women and men are estranged from each other; . . . children die!

This is abhorrent!

We condemn the abuses of Earth's ecosystems.

We condemn the poverty that stifles life's potential; the hunger that weakens the human body; the economic disparities that threaten so many families with ruin.

We condemn the social disarray of the nations; the disregard for justice which pushes citizens to the margin; the anarchy overtaking our communities; and the insane death of children from violence. In particular we condemn aggression and hatred in the name of religion.

But this agony need not be.

It need not be because the basis for an ethic already exists. This ethic offers the possibility of a better individual and global order, and leads individuals away from despair and societies away from chaos.

We are women and men who have embraced the precepts and practices of the world's religions.

We the People

We affirm that a common set of core values is found in the teachings of the religions, and that these form the basis of a global ethic.

We affirm that this truth is already known, but yet to be lived in heart and action.

We affirm that there is an irrevocable, unconditional norm for all areas of life, for families and communities, for races, nations and religions. There already exist ancient guidelines for human behavior which are found in the teachings of the religions of the world and which are the conditions for a sustainable world order.

We declare:

We are interdependent. Each of us depends on the well-being of the whole, and so we have respect for the community of living beings, for people, animals, and plants, and for the preservation of Earth, the air, water and soil.

We take individual responsibility for all we do. All our decisions, actions, and failures to act have consequences.

We must treat others as we wish others to treat us. We make a commitment to respect life and dignity, individuality and diversity, so that every person is treated humanely, without exception. We must have patience and acceptance. We must be able to forgive, learning from the past but never allowing ourselves to be enslaved by memories of hate. Opening our heart to one another, we must sink our narrow differences for the cause of world community, practicing a culture of solidarity and relatedness.

We consider humankind our family. We must strive to be kind and generous. We must not live for ourselves alone, but should also serve others, never forgetting the children, the aged, the poor, the suffering, the disabled, the refugees, and the lonely. No person should ever be considered or treated as a second-class citizen, or be exploited in any way whatsoever. There should be equal partnership between men and women. We must not commit any kind of sexual immorality. We must put behind us all forms of domination or abuse.

345

We commit ourselves to a culture of non-violence, respect, justice and peace. We shall not oppress, injure, torture, or kill other human beings, forsaking violence as a means of settling differences.

We must strive for a just social and economic order, in which everyone has an equal chance to reach full potential as a human being. We must speak and act truthfully and with compassion, dealing fairly with all, and avoiding prejudice and hatred. We must not steal. We must move beyond the dominance of greed for power, prestige, money and consumption to make a just and peaceful world. Earth cannot be changed for the better unless the consciousness of individuals is changed first. We pledge to increase our awareness by disciplining our minds, by meditation, by prayer, or by positive thinking. Without risk and a readiness to sacrifice there can be no fundamental change in our situation. Therefore we commit ourselves to this global ethic, to understanding one another, and to socially beneficial, peace-fostering, and nature-friendly ways of life.

We invite all people, whether religious or not, to do the same.

346

We, the Governments participating in the Fourth World Conference on Women,

Determined to advance the goals of equality, development and peace for all women everywhere in the interest of all humanity,

Acknowledging the voices of all women everywhere and taking note of the diversity of women and their roles and circumstances, honoring the women who paved the way and inspired by the hope present in the world's youth,

Recognize that the status of women has advanced in some important respects in the past decade but that progress has been uneven, inequalities between women and men have persisted and major obstacles remain, with serious consequences for the well-being of all people,

Also recognize that this situation is exacerbated by the increasing poverty that is affecting the lives of the majority of the world's people, in particular women and children, with origins in both the national and international domains,

Dedicate ourselves unreservedly to addressing these constraints and obstacles and thus enhancing further the advancement and empowerment of women all over the world, and agree that this requires urgent action in the spirit of determination, hope, cooperation and solidarity, now and to carry us forward into the next century.

benchmark draft of
The Earth Charter, 1998
*in preparation by representatives from around
the world for adoption by the United Nations*

347

Earth is our home and home to all living beings. Earth itself is alive. We are part of an evolving universe. Human beings are members of an interdependent community of life with a magnificent diversity of life forms and cultures. We are humbled before the beauty of Earth and share a reverence for life and the sources of our being. We give thanks for the heritage that we have received from past generations and embrace our responsibilities to present and future generations.

The Earth Community stands at a defining moment. The biosphere is governed by laws that we ignore at our own peril. Human beings have acquired the ability to radically alter the environment and evolutionary processes. Lack of foresight and misuse of knowledge and power threaten the fabric of life and the foundations of local and global security. There is great violence, poverty, and suffering in our world. A fundamental change of course is needed.

The choice is before us: to care for Earth or to participate in the destruction of ourselves and the diversity of life. We must reinvent industrial-technological civilization, finding new ways to balance self and community, having and being, diversity and unity, short-term and long-term, using and nurturing. In the midst of all our diversity, we are one humanity and one Earth family with a shared destiny. The challenges before us require an inclusive ethical vision. Partnerships must be forged and cooperation fostered at local, bioregional, national and international levels. In solidarity with one another and the community of life, we the peoples of the world commit ourselves to action guided by the following interrelated principles:

348

1. Respect Earth and all life. Earth, each life form, and all living beings possess intrinsic value and warrant respect independently of their utilitarian value to humanity.

2. Care for Earth, protecting and restoring the diversity, integrity, and beauty of the planet's ecosystems. Where there is risk of irreversible or serious damage to the environment, precautionary action must be taken to prevent harm.

3. Live sustainably, promoting and adopting modes of consumption, production and reproduction that respect and safeguard human rights and the regenerative capacities of Earth.

4. Establish justice, and defend without discrimination the right of all people to life, liberty, and security of person within an environment adequate for human health and spiritual well-being. People have a right to potable water, clean air, uncontaminated soil, and food security.

5. Share equitably the benefits of natural resource use and a healthy environment among the nations, between rich and poor, between males and females, between present and future generations, and internalize all environmental, social and economic costs.

6. Promote social development and financial systems that create and maintain sustainable livelihoods, eradicate poverty, and strengthen local communities.

7. Practice non-violence, recognizing that peace is the wholeness created by harmonious and balanced relation-

ships with oneself, other persons, other life forms, and
Earth.

8. Strengthen processes that empower people to participate
effectively in decision-making and ensure transparency
and accountability in governance and administration in
all sectors of society.

9. Reaffirm that Indigenous and Tribal Peoples have a vital
role in the care and protection of Mother Earth. They
have the right to retain their spirituality, knowledge,
lands, territories and resources.

10. Affirm that gender equality is a prerequisite for sustainable development.

11. Secure the right to sexual and reproductive health, with
special concern for women and girls.

12. Promote the participation of youth as accountable agents
of change for local, bioregional and global sustainability.

13. Advance and put to use scientific and other types of
knowledge and technologies that promote sustainable
living and protect the environment.

14. Ensure that people throughout their lives have opportunities to acquire the knowledge, values, and practical
skills needed to build sustainable communities.

15. Treat all creatures with compassion and protect them
from cruelty and wanton destruction.

16. Do not do to the environment of others what you do not
want done to your environment.

17. Protect and restore places of outstanding ecological, cultural, aesthetic, spiritual, and scientific significance.

18. Cultivate and act with a sense of shared responsibility
for the well-being of the Earth Community. Every person, institution and government has a duty to advance

the indivisible goals of justice for all, sustainability, world peace, and respect and care for the larger community of life.

Embracing the values in this Charter, we can grow into a family of cultures that allows the potential of all persons to unfold in harmony with the Earth Community. We must preserve a strong faith in the possibilities of the human spirit and a deep sense of belonging to the universe. Our best actions will embody the integration of knowledge with compassion.

In order to develop and implement the principles in this Charter, the nations of the world should adopt as a first step an international convention that provides an integrated legal framework for existing and future environmental and sustainable development law and policy.

INDEX OF AUTHORS

Index of Authors

353

ACKNOWLEDGMENTS

Most of the pieces in *Prayers for a Thousand Years* were written especially for this project and permission for them to be printed here was graciously given by their authors, who retain copyright. Permission inquiries to reprint these contributed pieces may be addressed to Elias Amidon and Elizabeth Roberts, c/o HarperSanFrancisco, 353 Sacramento Street, Suite 500, San Francisco, CA 94111.

Some authors, in response to the call for prayers and reflections for this project, sent material that had been previously published. These, along with about three dozen pieces that were gathered from published works, are noted below. Inquiries to reprint any of the following works should be directed to the publishers or authors cited.

Grateful acknowledgment is made for permission to reprint material copyrighted by the following authors or publishers:

Diane Ackerman. "School Prayer," by Diane Ackerman; contributed by the author. From *I Praise My Destroyer* by Diane Ackerman. Copyright © 1988 by Diane Ackerman. Reprinted by permission of Random House, Inc.

Margot Adler. From *Drawing Down the Moon* by Margot Adler. Copyright © 1979 by Margot Adler. Reprinted by permission of Viking Penguin, a division of Penguin Putnam Inc.

Nadja Awad. "Vision of a River," by Nadja Awad. 1998 "River of Words" Poetry Finalist. Age 15, Sana'a International School, Yemen. Reprinted by permission of International Rivers Network.

Bartholomew I. Excerpt from address given by Bartholomew I at the Symposium on the Sacredness of the Environment, 1997. Reprinted by permission of the Ecumenical Throne.

Holly St. John Bergon. Excerpt from "Of Rain Forests and Rivers," by Holly St. John Bergon. Copyright © by Holly St. John Bergon. From *Terra Nova*. Reprinted by permission of MIT Press Journals.

Wendell Berry. Excerpts from "Feminism, the Body, and the Machine" from *What Are People For?* by Wendell Berry. Copyright © 1990 by Wendell Berry. Reprinted by permission of North Point Press, a division of Farrar, Straus & Giroux, Inc.

Acknowledgments

Noah Frank. "I Want to Be," by Noah Frank. 1998 "River of Words" National Grand Prize Winner. Grade 2, Lakeshore Elementary School, San Francisco, CA. Reprinted by permission of International Rivers Network.

Damia Gates. "I Am," by Damia Gates. 1998 "River of Words" Poetry Finalist. Grade 4, Allendale Elementary School, Pasadena, CA. Reprinted by permission of International Rivers Network.

Maria Mazziotti Gillan. From *Where I Come From: New and Selected Poems,* (Guernica, 1995, 1997). Copyright © 1995 by Maria Mazziotti Gillan; contributed by the author. Reprinted by permission of the author.

Joy Harjo. "Remember," by Joy Harjo. From *She Had Some Horses.* Copyright © 1993 by Joy Harjo. Reprinted by permission of the author.

Václav Havel. Excerpt from *Letters to Olga,* by Václav Havel, page 369. Copyright © 1989 by Václav Havel. Reprinted by permission of Henry Holt & Co.

Anne Hillman. Excerpt from *The Dancing Animal Woman—A Celebration of Life,* by Anne Hillman. Copyright © 1994 by Anne Hillman. Reprinted by permission of author. Published by Bramble Books, Las Vegas, NV.

Jane Hirshfield. "Jasmine," from *The Lives of the Heart* by Jane Hirschfield. Copyright © 1997 by Jane Hirshfield. Reprinted by permission of HarperCollins Publishers.

Rolf Jacobsen. "When They Sleep," by Rolf Jacobsen; translated by Glen Storhaug. From *Night Open: Selected Poems of Rolf Jacobsen,* page 83. Copyright © 1993 by Rolf Jacobsen. Reprinted by permission of Glen Storhaug. Originally published in *Hemmelig Liv* by Gyldendal Norsk Forlag ASA.

Marilyn Krysl. "Why You Can't Sleep," by Marilyn Krysl; contributed by author. Copyright © by Marilyn Krysl. Reprinted by permission of author.

Aung San Suu Kyi. Excerpt from "Towards a Culture of Peace and Development," by Aung San Suu Kyi. From *Yes to a Global Ethic.* Copyright © 1996 by Aung San Suu Kyi. Reprinted by permission of The Continuum Publishing Company.

Marianne Larsen. "Ordinary Human Arms," by Marianne Larsen. Copyright © 1994 by Marianne Larsen. From *Poetry Like Bread.* Reprinted by permission of Curbstone Press.

Ursula Le Guin. "Initiation Song from the Finders Lodge," from *Always Coming Home,* by Ursula Le Guin. Copyright © 1985 by Ursula Le Guin. Reprinted by permission of HarperCollins Publishers.

Denise Levertov. From "Beginners," in *Candles in Babylon* (New York: New Directions Publishing Corp., 1982).

Mzwakhe Mbuli. "Now is the Time," by Mzwakhe Mbuli. From *Before Dawn.* Copyright © 1980 by Mzwakhe Mbuli. Reprinted by permission of Lester Brown & Associates.

Bill McKibben. Excerpt from *Hope, Human and Wild*, by Bill McKibben; contributed by author. Copyright © 1996 by Bill McKibben. Reprinted by permission of Little, Brown and Co.

W. S. Merwin. "Thanks," by W. S. Merwin. From *The Rain in the Trees*. Copyright © 1988 by W. S. Merwin. Reprinted by permission of Alfred A. Knopf, Inc.

Stephanie Mills. Excerpt from *In Service of the Wild: Restoring and Reinhabiting Damaged Land,* by Stephanie Mills; contributed by the author. Copyright © 1995 by Stephanie Mills. Reprinted by permission of Beacon Press.

Stephan Mitchell. "Psalm 24" from *A Book of Psalms* by Stephan Mitchell. Copyright © 1993 by Stephan Mitchell. Reprinted by permission of Harper-Collins Publishers.

N. Scott Momaday. From *In the Bear's House,* by N. Scott Momaday, page 33; contributed by the author. Copyright © 1999 by N. Scott Momaday. Reprinted by permission of St. Martin's Press, Inc.

Pablo Neruda. From *2000* by Pablo Neruda. Copyright © 1992 by Pablo Neruda. Translated by Richard Schaaf. Reprinted by permission of Azul Editions.

Nun's 23rd Psalm. From *Guide My Feet* by Marian Wright Edelman. Copyright © 1995 by Marian Wright Edelman. Reprinted by permission of All Saints Convent, Catonville, Maryland.

Sharon Olds. "Summer Solstice, New York City" by Sharon Olds; contributed by the author. From *The Gold Cell*. Copyright © 1987 by Sharon Olds. Reprinted by permission of Alfred. A. Knopf, Inc.

Mary Oliver. "The Journey," by Mary Oliver. From *Dream Work*. Copyright © 1986 by Mary Oliver. Reprinted by permission of Grove/Atlantic, Inc.

Simon Ortiz. From *Woven Stone* by Simon Ortiz, University of Arizona Press. Copyright © 1992 by Simon Ortiz. Reprinted by permission of the author.

Alicia Ostriker. "A Prayer to the Shekhina," by Alicia Ostriker. Copyright © 1994 by Alicia Ostriker; contributed by the author. From *The Nakedness of the Fathers: Biblical Visions and Revisions,* Rutgers University Press, 1994. Reprinted by permission of author.

Marge Piercy. "To Be of Use," by Marge Piercy. From *Circles on the Water*. Copyright © 1982 by Marge Piercy. Reprinted by permission of Alfred A. Knopf, Inc.

Sandra Postel and Christopher Flavin. "Reshaping the Global Economy. From *Celebrating Earth Holy Days*. Copyright © by Sandra Postel and

Christopher Flavin. Reprinted by permission of The Crossroad Publishing Company.

Daniel Quinn. From *Providence: The Story of a Fifty-Year Vision Quest;* contributed by the author. Copyright © 1996 by Daniel Quinn. Reprinted by permission of Bantam Books, a division of Random House, Inc.

Finley Schaef and Elizabeth Dyson. From vision statement for North American Coalition for Christianity and Ecology (NACCE). Copyright © by Finley Schaef and Elizabeth Dyson. Reprinted by permission of authors.

Sr. Mary Rosita Shiosse. "A Liturgy for the Earth," by Sister Mary Rosita Shiosse. From *Celebrating Earth Holy Days.* Copyright © by Sr. Mary Rosita Shiosse. Reprinted by permission of The Crossroad Publishing Company.

Gary Snyder. "In the Next Century," by Gary Snyder. From *Turtle Island.* Copyright © 1974 by Gary Snyder. Reprinted by permission of New Directions Publishing Corp.

Starhawk. "Declaration of the Four Sacred Things," by Starhawk; contributed by the author. From *The Fifth Sacred Thing* by Miriam (Starhawk) Simos. Copyright © 1993 by Miriam Simos. Reprinted by permission of Bantam Books, a division of Random House, Inc.

Masika Szilagy. "Ten Thousand Years" from *The Holy Book of Women's Mysteries* by Masika Szilagy. Copyright © by daughter Zsuzsanna Budapest, www.netwiz.net.

Nicole Thibodeaux. 1996 "River of Words" First Place Winner. Grade 10, Taos High School, Pilar, NM. Reprinted by permission of International Rivers Network.

Nguyen Cong Tru.From *The Miracle of Mindfulness, by* Thich Nhat Hanh. Copyright © 1975 byThich Nhat Hanh.

Amy Uyematsu. Excerpt from "Stone, Bow, Prayer," by Amy Uyematsu; contributed by author. Copyright © 1998 by Amy Uyematsu. Full poem published by *Luna.*

Michael Ventura. From *The Sun*, Nov. 1997. Copyright © 1996 by Michael Ventura. Reprinted by permission of the author.

Alma Luz Villanueva. "Dear World," by Alma Luz Villanueva. From *Desire,* page 138; contributed by author. Copyright © 1998 by Alma Luz Villaneuva. Reprinted by permission of Bilingual Press/Editorial Bilingüe, Arizona State University, Tempe, AZ.

Alice Walker. "We Have a Beautiful Mother," from *Her Blue Body. Everything We Know: Earthling Poemss, 1965–1990.* Copyright © 1991 by Alice Walker. Reprinted by permission of Harcourt Brace and Company.

Acknowledgments

Women's Environment and Development Organization (WEDO). "A Women's Creed, The Declaration of the Women's Global Strategies Meeting," 1994, written by Robin Morgan, in collaboration with Perdita Huston, Sunetra Puri, Mahnaz Afkhami, Diane Faulkner, Corrine Kumar, Simla Wali, and Paola Melchiori.

David Whyte. "Enough," by David Whyte. From *Where Many Rivers Meet*. Copyright © 1990 by David Whyte. Reprinted by permission of Many Rivers Press.

An exhaustive effort has been made to locate all rights holders and to clear reprint permissions. If any required acknowledgments have been omitted, or any rights overlooked, the publishers will be pleased, once notified, to rectify any omission in future editions.

360